Caoicno Meulean
99 Newmarket
Lansdale

The Pastoral Epistles

The Pastoral Epistles

A Digest of Reformed Comment

GEOFFREY B. WILSON

MINISTER OF BIRKBY BAPTIST CHURCH
HUDDERSFIELD

THE BANNER OF TRUTH TRUST

THE BANNER OF TRUTH TRUST
3 Murrayfield Road, Edinburgh EH12 6EL
PO Box 621, Carlisle, Pennsylvania 17013, USA

★

© Geoffrey Backhouse Wilson 1982
First published 1982
ISBN 0 85151 335 2

★

Filmset, printed and bound in Great Britain by
Hazell Watson & Viney Ltd, Aylesbury, Bucks

TO THE REV. AND MRS. W. R. MARTIN
WITH LOVE AND GRATITUDE

CONTENTS

PREFACE

It is hoped that this brief treatment of the Pastorals may prove helpful to busy people. I would like to thank the publishers who have kindly given permission to quote from their works, and Dr. Williams's Library for the extended loan of various books. The commentary is based on the American Standard Version (1901), published by Thomas Nelson Inc.

Huddersfield   GEOFFREY WILSON
July 1981

PREFACE

INTRODUCTION

Since the eighteenth century, the letters to Timothy and Titus have been known as the 'Pastoral' Epistles, because they are largely concerned with the duties of those who are called to lead the flock of God. Unlike the anonymous Epistle to the Hebrews, these letters not only bear Paul's name, but are addressed to two of his most trusted assistants. As the apostolic authorship is amply supported by both the external and internal evidence, the authenticity of the Pastorals did not become a 'problem' until the rise of modern scepticism. The five arguments advanced against their genuineness have centred upon (1) the historical setting, (2) the ecclesiastical situation, (3) the doctrinal viewpoint, (4) the heresy condemned, and (5) the linguistic differences.

It is arbitrary to dismiss the *historical data* contained in these Epistles on the assumption that the execution of Paul took place at the end of his two-year imprisonment in Rome, for the triumphant conclusion of Acts suggests vindication rather than martyrdom [*Acts* 28.30, 31], and this view is confirmed by Paul's own expectations of an early release from captivity [*Phil* 1.25; 2.24; *Philemon* 22]. Although the sequence of Paul's movements after he was set free is problematical, it would appear that he travelled east before making his long awaited trip to Spain [*Rom*

15.23, 24]. If we assume that he was released in AD 63, Paul may have visited Crete on the way to Ephesus and Colossae, and then returned through Macedonia for a stay at Philippi before proceeding to Nicopolis, where he spent the winter. A mission to Spain of at least a year probably followed in the Spring of AD 64, but when we next hear of Paul he is again in Asia Minor. It is possible that Paul was re-arrested after further ministry in Ephesus, for the journey back to Rome seems to have been via Miletus, Troas, and Corinth [2 *Tim* 4. 13, 20]. Amid all these uncertainties, we can at least be sure that Paul wrote 1 *Timothy* and *Titus* while he was still at liberty, and 2 *Timothy* during his final imprisonment in Rome [c. AD 67]. Hence the commentary follows this order.

There is no ground for supposing that the *ecclesiastical situation* reflected in the Pastorals requires a date later than the lifetime of Paul. By the time of Ignatius [c. AD 115] a resident bishop exercised authority over the elders and deacons of the local church, but here there are only two orders of ministry, for the terms 'bishop' and 'elder' are still used interchangeably as they are in *Acts* [20.17, 28; cf *Titus* 1.5, 7]. Moreover, Timothy and Titus clearly have a roving commission to act as the apostle's personal representatives to the churches, and are not monarchical bishops after the second-century pattern. Directions are given for the enrolling of widows worthy of the church's support, but the existence of an official 'order' of widows cannot be proved from the passage [1 *Tim* 5.3–16].

A further difficulty concerns the difference in the *doctrinal viewpoint* of these letters. Critics adversely compare the continued stress upon the need to maintain orthodoxy ('*the* faith' as a deposit rather than 'faith' in Christ) and piety ('godliness') with the striking originality of Paul's thought. But as A. Sabatier observed, 'Paul was an apostle before he was a theologian. To him the need of conservation was more urgent than that of innovation. His gospel was, above everything else, a message that he had received, and that he had to deliver and defend' [cf 1 *Cor* 15.1–11; *Gal* 1.6–9; 2 *Thess* 2.15]. It should therefore occasion no surprise to find that Paul's parting counsels emphasize the importance of preserving the apostolic gospel in both purity of doctrine and of life.

There is now little support for identifying the *heresy condemned* with the fully developed Gnostic systems of the second century. The error seems to reflect a Jewish form of incipient gnosticism, not unlike but not more advanced than the false teaching which is refuted in the Colossian Epistle. The Judaistic origin of this deviation from the faith is proved by the references to the law, circumcision, genealogies, and 'Jewish fables' [1 *Tim* 1.7; *Titus* 1.10, 14; 3.9], while pagan influences apparently led to a dualistic understanding of the world which would account for the ascetic prohibition of marriage and certain foods [1 *Tim* 4.3–5; *Titus* 1.14, 15]. Presumably the belief that the 'resurrection is already past' [2 *Tim* 2.18] was due to the same proto-gnostic tendency to spiritualize what was a fundamental article of Christian belief [1 *Cor* 15.20].

But the major objection to the Pauline authorship centres upon the *linguistic differences* between the Pastorals and other Pauline Epistles. Although much has been made of the occurrence of 306 words which are not found elsewhere in Paul's writings, it is quite unreasonable to deny Paul their use when critics admit that the 2,177 words of the other ten Epistles do not represent the apostle's entire vocabulary (Donald Guthrie). Moreover, it is surely self-evident that different subjects call for different modes of expression. As we do not demand that Shakespeare's *Sonnets* should exhibit a certain percentage of *Hamlet* words, 'we should not expect that an author's favourite expressions would be distributed over the pages of his book like the spots on a wall-paper pattern' (Newport J. D. White). It should also be recognized that the probable quotation of much traditional material (including confessions of faith, and doxologies or hymns) accounts for many of the stylistic peculiarities of these Epistles.

Those who suppose the Pastorals to be the spurious productions of a post-apostolic imitator are encased in the problems of their own making. 'If there are difficulties in vindicating the Pauline authorship, it is still more difficult to prove in whole or in part how a forger could manufacture three such Epistles as these are, in form and contents, and foist them on the Apostle Paul' (J. E. Huther). The gravest ethical questions are raised by the refusal to receive the Epistles as Paul's authentic utterances. For the denial of their apostolic origin demands the invention of so many personal allusions and circumstantial details as to make their fabricator's professed concern for the truth nothing less than a piece of consummate hypocrisy. Although the term 'pseudonymous' may lend a certain dignity to the deception, it does not remove the moral difficulty, and it is far more realistic 'to assume that an author's own claims are valid unless they are psychologically improbable' (Guthrie). We have briefly tried to show that there are very good grounds for maintaining that Paul was in fact the author of these farewell letters to Timothy and Titus, but perhaps the most impressive proof of their apostolicity may be seen in the immense gulf which separates them from the pathetically pedestrian literature of the second century.

1 TIMOTHY

CHAPTER ONE

Paul greets Timothy as his true child in the faith, and exhorts him to refute the irrelevant myths and genealogies spread by those who want to be teachers of the law, for they are as ignorant of the meaning of the law as they are of the glorious gospel which was committed to the apostle [vv 1–11]. As a former persecutor Paul is a conspicuous example of the divine mercy, and he praises God for calling him to preach Christ, who came into the world to save sinners [vv 12–17]. Accordingly Timothy is urged to remain faithful to his commission, and is warned of such men as Hymenaeus and Alexander, who have made shipwreck of their faith [vv 18–20].

V 1: **Paul, an apostle of Christ Jesus according to the commandment of God our Saviour, and Christ Jesus our hope;**

This is not merely a private letter to a faithful helper, for the official character of the address shows that Paul intended it to be read to the church at Ephesus, where he had left Timothy to act as his representative in dealing with the threat posed to the faith by false teachers [*v* 3]. In introducing himself as 'an apostle' ('one sent forth') of Christ Jesus, Paul is clearly using the word in its highest sense, since he is one of that select company who received the gospel from the Lord himself [*Gal* 1.12]. 'The distinguishing features of an apostle were, a commission directly from Christ: being a witness of the resurrection: special inspiration: supreme authority: accrediting by miracles: unlimited commission to preach and to found churches' (Marvin Vincent). The order 'Christ Jesus' is more frequent in Paul, particularly in the Pastorals (25 times), perhaps because his experience began with the revelation of Christ's heavenly glory; whereas 'Jesus Christ' is the form favoured by writers like Peter and John, who had come to faith in the Messiah through a knowledge of his earthly life.

according to the commandment of God our Saviour, and Christ Jesus our hope; The linking together of God and Christ as the co-ordinate sources of Paul's apostleship is highly significant, for it gives clear evidence of his belief in the deity of Christ. At the outset of a letter which combats false teaching, Paul is careful to emphasize that he is not a self-appointed teacher of his own ideas, but is sent forth to preach the gospel by the command of God 'our Saviour' and Christ Jesus 'our hope'. The confessional 'our' is itself an appeal to the Ephesian church not to exchange the verities of the gospel for the vain myths of men. The title 'Saviour' is applied to God six times in the Pastorals, and this shows that God's free offer of salvation must be extended to all men, in contrast to the exclusive claims of the false teachers who limited salvation to those who had the superior discernment to join their clique. As God is the author of our salvation, so Christ is the embodiment of our hope. Our risen and glorified Lord is himself our hope, because his triumph over sin and death provides the objective pledge of our final redemption [*Phil* 3.20,21; *Col* 1.27; 1 *John* 3.2].

*V*2: **unto Timothy, my true child in faith: Grace, mercy, peace, from God the Father and Christ Jesus our Lord.**

Paul warmly addresses Timothy as his true spiritual child whom he has begotten in the sphere of faith. Timothy was converted through Paul's ministry at Lystra, and later became a constant companion of the apostle [*Acts* 16.1–3]. According to tradition, Timothy was martyred by a mob at Ephesus in AD 97 for opposing the licentious idolatry of the cult of Diana. In greeting Timothy [cf 2 *Tim* 1.2], Paul appropriately adds 'mercy' to his usual 'grace' and 'peace', since the experience of the divine mercy 'produces fitness for the Gospel ministry, *vv* 13, 16; 2 *Cor* 4.1; I *Cor* 7.25' (J. A. Bengel). As ministers commend the mercy of God to others, they must never forget that they need to be partakers of it themselves. 'If they know aright what they are, and what they should be, they will be ever throwing themselves on God's mercy' (Patrick Fairbairn). 'Grace' is God's undeserved favour in forgiving sinners, as 'mercy' is his spontaneous compassion in freeing them from the misery entailed by their disobedience, while 'peace' is that aspect of salvation which results from an experience of this grace and mercy. Thus God extends his 'grace' to men as they are *guilty*, and his 'mercy' to them as they are *miserable* (R. C. Trench). In the final clause Paul again emphasizes the divine dignity of Christ by showing that this triple blessing is conjointly bestowed by 'God the Father and Christ Jesus our Lord'.

*V*3: **As I exhorted thee to tarry at Ephesus, when I was going into Macedonia, that thou mightest charge certain men not to teach a different doctrine, 4 neither to give heed to fables and endless genealogies, which minister questionings, rather than a dispensation of God which is in faith;** *so do I now.*

I write to thee now, **as I exhorted thee to tarry at Ephesus, when I was going into Macedonia,** It is probably better to supply what Paul leaves unexpressed at the beginning of verse 3 rather than at the end of verse 4 as in the ASV ('*so do I now*'). Upon his release from Rome, Paul sent Timothy to Philippi to find out how the church there was faring [*Phil* 2.19], and evidently arranged to meet Timothy at Ephesus after returning from Colossae. As Paul was anxious to fulfil his promise to visit Philippi [*Phil* 2.24], he delegated the task of dealing with the false teachers at Ephesus to Timothy, and he now writes to confirm this commission so that none can question the authority of his representative.

that thou mightest charge certain men not to teach a different doctrine, neither to give heed to fables and endless genealogies, No doubt Paul knew the identity of those responsible for introducing these alien novelties, but his refusal to name them was probably intended to avoid giving such would-be 'teachers of the law' [*v* 7] any standing in the community of faith. In this Jewish teaching the gospel of God's free grace was displaced by fanciful myths and interminable genealogies, not unlike the unwholesome allegorical inventions found in Philo or the apocalyptic Book of Jubilees [cf 4.7; *Titus* 1.14; 3.9].

they promote useless speculations rather than divine training that is in faith. (Arndt-Gingrich) Here it would seem that the word *oikonomia* ('dispensation') should be taken in the subjective sense of training in the way of salvation. Paul judges this teaching by its results. He brands such empty arguments as 'useless speculations,' because they cannot promote the godly discipline which accompanies faith.

*V*5: **But the end of the charge is love out of a pure heart and a good conscience and faith unfeigned:**

In contrast to the false teaching which results in strife and sterile questionings, the goal of the charge given by Timothy to the church at Ephesus is the love which can only spring from a real experience of the grace of God. Instead of pointing to the divine origin of this love [*Rom* 5.5], Paul here gives a threefold description of its proximate source, because he wishes to stress the inner sincerity which always distinguishes a genuine profession from its plausible counterfeits. 1. *A pure heart*. In Scripture 'the heart' stands for the totality of man's innermost self [*Prov* 4.23], and so 'a pure heart' points to the radical inward renewal which enables a man to love and serve God with single-minded devotion [*Matt* 5.8; 2 *Tim* 2.22]. 2. *A good conscience*. The word 'conscience', literally means 'a knowing with', and is the term frequently used by Paul to designate that innate faculty of self-judgment by which a man tries his own thoughts and actions [*Rom* 2.15]. To experience freedom from the guilt of sin and be led by the Spirit is to enjoy the blessing of a 'good' conscience, but no testimony is given by the 'branded' or 'seared' conscience of those who have rejected the truth in favour of

Satan's lies [4.2]. 3. *Faith unfeigned*. With a sidelong glance at the false teachers, Paul speaks of the 'unhypocritical' faith which needs no actor's mask to conceal its insincerity [2 *Tim* 1.5]. For instead of the true faith which works by love and thus fulfils the law [*Rom* 13.10; *Gal* 5.6], theirs was a faith which drew men into profitless speculations and vain talking [*vv* 4,6].

V6: from which things some having swerved have turned aside unto vain talking;

It was from this triad of graces that the false teachers had wandered away, having missed the goal by turning off into meaningless chatter. The secret of much unsatisfactory and unprofitable preaching is disclosed by the folly of these men. Since they had not the root of the matter in them, 'they naturally fell to discoursing about vain questions, the debatable and speculative points about which they *could* find themselves at home . . . If the heart is not *in* the great things of the gospel, if it is out of accord with their deep spiritual tone, it cannot delight to speak of them, and will be only too glad to turn aside to inferior topics' (Fairbairn).

V7: desiring to be teachers of the law, though they understand neither what they say, nor whereof they confidently affirm.

The errorists wanted to be teachers of the law, but as they had no insight into the meaning of the law and its relationship to the gospel [*v* 8], they did not know what they were saying and could not grasp the things about which they spoke with such superficial confidence. The same feature may be observed in all those who deviate from the truth of the gospel. They announce their errors with the stubborn assurance that is born of ignorance!

*V*8: **But we know that the law is good, if a man use it lawfully,**

In case his disparaging reference to 'teachers of the law' should appear to reflect upon the law itself, Paul immediately adds that the law is good [*Rom* 7.12, 16], provided it is used lawfully. This deliberate play on words is very much to the point. 'The law itself, because it is law, dictates its lawful use and condemns every abuse as being unlawful. All pretending law teachers stand condemned by the very law they pretend to teach' (R. C. H. Lenski). The would-be law teachers in Ephesus swerved from the path of truth when they made the law the spring-board for their fanciful interpretations. Confusing the law with the gospel, they could not see that the law was given primarily to bring sin to light and condemn evil-doers. Paul's standpoint here is in complete accord with the teaching of the great evangelical Epistles [cf *Rom* 7.7–25; *Gal* 3.19–25]. Since the law was added 'for the sake of transgressions', it is designed not for a righteous man, but 'for the lawless and unruly' [*v* 9]. And because Timothy knows this, he will know how to 'use the law', 'not in Jewish fashion as a yoke for the saint, but as a whip for the sinner' (George G. Findlay).

*V*9: **as knowing this, that law is not made for a righteous man, but for the lawless and unruly, for the ungodly and sinners, for the unholy and profane, for murderers of fathers and murderers of mothers,**

for manslayers, 10 **for fornicators, for abusers of themselves with men, for men-stealers, for liars, for false swearers, and if there be any other thing contrary to the sound doctrine;** 11 **according to the gospel of the glory of the blessed God, which was committed to my trust.**

Against the mixture of law-teaching and licence championed by the errorists, Paul lays down the general principle that the law was not made for a 'righteous' man. Although this word is used in its widest sense, the believer is evidently in view. Unlike the wicked, the Christian is no longer under the condemning power of the law, because he now desires to act in conformity with its requirements [cf *Rom* 8.1–4; *Gal* 5.23]. In a characteristic enumeration Paul sets forth the positive function of the law. The list follows the order of the Ten Commandments. The first three pairs cover offences against God, while the vices mentioned are all violations of the second table of the law. 'In each case extreme forms of the sin are chosen to emphasize the strength of evil in the heathen world and the real need of law for those who have not heard of the gospel: cf *Rom* 1.21–32' (Walter Lock).

but for the lawless and unruly, The active enmity of sinners towards God is demonstrated in their refusal to acknowledge the Creator's lordship over them. When dependent creatures thus assert their own autonomy, they choose that self-determination which inevitably leads to self-destruction, since the disobedient cannot escape the awful punishment threatened by the law they have despised. The distinction between the two terms is well noted by Marvin Vincent: 'In the one case no legal obligation is recognized; in the other, subjection to law is refused'.

for the ungodly and sinners, These are very properly linked together, because the man who is without inward reverence for God always reveals his defiance in many outward acts of rebellion, and so deliberately falls short of the true goal of his existence (cf. *The Shorter Catechism*, Answer to Question 1: 'Man's chief end is to glorify God, and to enjoy him for ever'). [1 *Pet* 4.18; *Jude* 15].

for the unholy and profane, Here the negative is again correctly combined with the positive, for the man to whom nothing is sacred has the same secular spirit as Esau, who sold his birthright for one miserable meal [*Heb* 12.16]. 'Profane' comes from the word 'threshold', and strictly means what may be trodden, hence unhallowed. The profane are therefore those 'who walk over everything and make it as common as dirt' (Lenski).

for smiters of fathers and smiters of mothers, (ASV margin) Probably the sin condemned is not parricide, but that of dishonouring parents. 'For this extreme and outrageous violation of the Fifth commandment the punishment of death was provided in the Mosaic law' (J. H. Bernard). [*Exod* 21.15].

for manslayers, Or murderers. Violators of the Sixth Commandment show a total disregard for the sanctity of life. As murder is the supreme manifestation of human hate and a direct assault upon the image of God in man, it is a crime for which the only appropriate punishment is death [*Num* 35.16]. 'It is the sanctity of life that validates the death penalty for the crime of murder' (John Murray, *Principles of Conduct*, p.122).

for immoral persons, sodomites, Persons guilty of two of the most repulsive breaches of the Seventh Commandment. Sexual laxity, especially as this is manifested in the perverted practice of sodomy, always heralds the decline of a civilization and is a certain mark of the wrath of God [*Rom* 1.18, 27]. Notwithstanding the modern churchmen who condone and even advocate homosexuality, Paul categorically states that none who indulge in such a vile sin shall inherit the kingdom of God [1 *Cor* 6.9].

for kidnappers, 'A man's most precious possession is *himself*, and the worst form of thieving (condemned in the Eighth Commandment) is that practised by slave-dealers, whose booty is not *things*, but *persons*' (Bernard) [*Exod* 21.16; *Deut* 24.7].

for liars, for false swearers, Those who break the Ninth Commandment usually contradict, distort, or suppress the truth to gain some dishonourable end, but the worst form of lying is that which is solemnly confirmed by an oath.

and if there be any other thing contrary to the sound doctrine; Paul rounds off the catalogue with an inclusive clause covering whatever else is contrary 'to the sound (or healthy) doctrine'. By his repeated use of this phrase, the apostle implicitly contrasts the cancerous teaching of the ignorant legalists with the wholesome influence of the gospel [2 *Tim* 4.3; *Titus* 1.9, 2.1].

according to the gospel of the glory of the blessed

[26]

God, This is loosely attached to the whole of the preceding statement concerning the place of the law in Christian instruction [*vv* 8–10]. The law subserves the interests of the gospel by restraining evil-doers and convicting them of their sin, but it must never be regarded as an essential supplement to the gospel, because justification does not come by our striving to render obedience to the law [*Acts* 13.39; *Rom* 3.20]. 'The gospel of God's glory is the gospel which peculiarly displays His glory – unfolds this to the view of men by showing the moral character and perfections of God exhibited as they are nowhere else in the person and work of Christ' (Fairbairn) [cf 2 *Cor* 4.4] On the expression 'the blessed God' (cf 6.15), Bengel succinctly remarks, 'The Blessed blesses'. As God contains all blessedness in himself, so he is the source of all blessing for men. 'The epithet seems added from the rush of personal feeling as the sense of the present love and mercy of Christ (never long absent) comes to him strongly in penning the words' (A. E. Humphreys).

which was committed to my trust. Or 'with which *I* was entrusted'. This is an essential reminder of Paul's authority, for it emphatically affirms his divine commission against the 'teachers of law' [*v* 7], and thus prepares the way for what follows [*vv* 12–14].

*V*12: **I thank him that enabled me, even Christ Jesus our Lord, for that he counted me faithful, appointing me to *his* service;**

Although at first sight this may only seem to be a personal aside, it is no mere digression, but is in fact an integral part of Paul's argument. For his own history not only provides a signal example of the divine mercy, but also illustrates the disastrous effects of legalistic zeal [v 13; Phil 3.6]. 'In a word, the law was for the *condemnation* of sinners, the gospel was for the *saving* of sinners and the ministration of forgiveness' (C. J. Ellicott). Hence Timothy must at once stop the pretended law-teachers, if the Ephesians are not to exchange the blessings of the gospel for the ministration of death. In this passage Paul speaks with such an intensity of feeling that his readers cannot fail to take the lesson to heart (see comment on verse 1). 'Here speaks the very soul of Paul. Here is doctrine turned into life. Past experience burns undimmed, confession of sin, confession of faith, gratefulness, burst into praise and doxology' (Lenski).

I thank him . . . As Paul can never forget the encounter on the way to Damascus which turned him into a preacher of the Faith he once persecuted, so he never ceases to be grateful to Christ who then enabled him, counted him trustworthy, and appointed him to his service. The proof of Christ's enabling was seen in the trust thus committed to Paul. 'He saith, *Christ enabled me*, that is, endowed him with fidelity, zeal, courage, and all other qualifications requisite for that honourable and difficult ministry, 2 Cor 3.5,6 . . . His faithfulness was not the cause or motive, but the fruit and effect, of the grace of God in calling him to the ministry. This he expressly declares, 1 Cor 7.25, *hath obtained mercy to be faithful*. If our Saviour had only discovered his fidelity, without bestowing that grace upon him, there had not been a reason of such affectionate thanksgiving; for that always supposes some favour and benefit received' (Matthew Poole).

service It is the mark of Paul's humility that he chooses to describe his vocation by the lowly word *diakonia*. Its use here clearly attests the apostolic authorship of the Pastorals, since no second-century writer would have applied to an apostle a term which was then associated with the service of deacons.

*V*13: **though I was before a blasphemer, and a persecutor, and injurious: howbeit I obtained mercy, because I did it ignorantly in unbelief;**

Paul's purpose in recalling his sinful past is to magnify the superabounding grace he was shown [*v* 14]. This self-indictment is arranged on an ascending scale: he was before 'a blasphemer' who denied Christ and forced others to do the same [*Acts* 26.11]; 'a persecutor' who by his relentless pursuit of the Lord's people persecuted the Lord himself [*Acts* 22.4, 7]; and 'injurious', being a man of violence with an outrageous disregard of other men's rights. Yet such a sinner still came within the scope of God's mercy, because he 'did it ignorantly in unbelief'. Guilty though he was, his unbelief was not a clear-eyed rejection of the truth [*Mark* 3.28–30], for he acted with the zeal which was not according to knowledge [*Acts* 26.9; *Rom* 10.2]. This ignorance was deeply culpable, but it was not unpardonable. For Jesus responded to the ignorance of his murderers with a prayer for mercy, and that was the mercy which overtook the persecutor on the road to Damascus [*Luke* 23.34].

*V*14: **and the grace of our Lord abounded exceedingly with faith and love which is in Christ Jesus.**

It was the conviction of the enormity of his transgressions that gave Paul this deep and abiding consciousness of the superabundance of the Lord's forgiving grace [v 15]. While a fanatical adherence to the law had made him the helpless prisoner of sin, grace alone brought the captive the new life of love and liberty which is found in union with Christ Jesus. This was something that those in Ephesus over whom the law was exerting the same fatal fascination would do well to bear in mind! 'He mentions *faith and love*, the two principal graces, in opposition to the reigning sins in his unconverted state: faith in the doctrine of the gospel, in opposition to his former ignorance and infidelity; and love to Christ and believers, in opposition to his former rage and cruelty against them' (Poole). It is worth noting that this verse, together with verse 15, was the origin of the title of John Bunyan's spiritual autobiography, *Grace Abounding to the Chief of Sinners*.

*V*15: **Faithful is the saying, and worthy of all acception, that Christ Jesus came into the world to save sinners; of whom I am chief:**

Faithful is the saying, This is the first of the five 'Faithful sayings' which are found in the Pastoral Epistles [1.15; 3.1; 4.9; *Titus* 3.8; 2 *Tim* 2.11]. It is significant that scarcely thirty years after the crucifixion Paul is thus able to remind his assistants of the gospel message by means 'of a body of utterances in which the essence of the gospel has been crystallized by those who have tasted and seen its preciousness. Obviously the days when this gospel was brought as a novelty to their attention are past . . . The gospel has been embraced and lived; it has been trusted and not found wanting; and the souls that have found its blessedness have had time to frame its precious truths into formulas . . . They are dug from the mine of the Christian heart indeed, but they come to us stamped in the mintage of apostolic authority' (B. B. Warfield, 'The Saving Christ' reprinted in *The Person and Work of Christ*, pp. 549–560).

and worthy of all acceptation, The primary thought here is not that the gospel is worthy to be accepted by all, but that it is deserving of 'complete acceptance in every way, without reservation, without hesitation, without the least doubt' (Lenski).

that Christ Jesus came into the world sinners to save; 'That' introduces the brief but marvellously full 'saying' which sums up the whole gospel in only eight Greek words. It is a joyful declaration of the purpose of Christ's coming into the world of sin and death. He descended into the sphere of evil for no other reason than to save poor lost sinners ('sinners' is placed before the verb for emphasis in the Greek). He who eternally existed in the form of God willingly took the form of a servant in order to die the death our sins deserved [cf *Phil* 2.5–11]. 'Jesus did all that is included in the great word '*save*'. He did not come to induce us to save ourselves, or to help us to save ourselves, or to enable us to save ourselves. He came to *save* us. And it is therefore that His name was called Jesus – because He should save His people from their sins. The glory of our Lord, surpassing all His other glories to usward, is just that He is our actual and complete Saviour; our Saviour to the uttermost' (Warfield, *op. cit.*, p. 557).

of whom I am chief: By at once applying the saying to himself, Paul responds to it in the same way he would have others respond to it (*v* 16). He says 'I am' and *not* 'I was', for though his sinful past has been blotted out by the mercy of God, he is acutely conscious of the fact that he is not yet made perfect (Phil 3.12). 'In the experiences of personal religion each individual man is alone with God. He sees nought but the Holy One and his own sinful self [cf *Luke* 18.13, *to me the sinner*]. And the more familiar a man becomes with the meeting of God face to face the less likely is he to be deceived as to the gulf which parts him, limited, finite, defective, from the Infinite and Perfect' (White).

V 16: **howbeit for this cause I obtained mercy, that in me as chief might Jesus Christ show forth all his longsuffering, for an ensample of them that should thereafter believe on him unto eternal life.**

But I was mercifully dealt with for this very purpose, that Jesus Christ might find in me the first occasion for displaying all his patience, (NEB) In the previous verse the word 'chief' (*prōtos*) signifies 'foremost in rank', but here it takes on the temporal meaning of 'first in time'. Such was the former persecutor's pre-eminence in sin that it served to demonstrate the full extent of Christ's patience. 'Greater longsuffering He could not show in any case than in mine, nor find a sinner that so required *all* His longsuffering; not a part only' (John Chrysostom).

for a pattern to them which should hereafter believe on him to life everlasting. (AV) Paul sees himself as a 'pattern', the 'prototype' or 'outline sketch' of the kind of sinners Jesus came to save. 'His meaning is that right from the very beginning God showed this example of His grace that could be seen clearly and widely, so that no one should doubt that if only he comes to Christ in faith, he may obtain pardon. All our distrust is removed when we see in Paul a visible type of that grace which we seek' (John Calvin). All who are saved by Christ 'believe *on* him *unto* eternal life' (ASV). This means that they continue to rest their faith on Christ until they attain eternal life, whereas temporary believers always reveal the falsity and inadequacy of their profession by falling short of the promised goal.

*V*17. **Now unto the King eternal, immortal, invisible, the only God,** *be* **honour and glory for ever and ever. Amen.**

The remembrance of the abounding grace he was shown prompts Paul to break forth into a fervent doxology [6.15; *Rom* 11.36]. 'The King eternal' literally means 'the King of the ages', and the title evidently springs from the Jewish view of the two ages, the present age and the age to come. 'God was King in both spheres, and indeed of the "ages of the ages" as the phrase *for ever and ever* suggests' (Donald Guthrie). The three adjectives – immortal, invisible, only – provide a striking description of the nature of God. Unlike mortal man, God is incorruptible and so immortal [cf *Rom* 1.23]. As God is also invisible, he is beyond human examination [6.16], and can be known only by those to whom he chooses to reveal himself [*Heb* 11.27]. And he is the *only* God as opposed to all the finite deities of man's invention [1 *Cor* 8.4, 5]. 'To Him alone belong honour and glory, and to Him they belong to all eternity' (Fairbairn). The liturgical 'Amen' ('So be it!') is an emphatic invitation to every believer to set his own seal to the truth thus affirmed.

*V*18: **This charge I commit unto thee, my child Timothy, according to the prophecies which led the way to thee, that by them thou mayest war the good warfare;**

In returning to the original charge given to Timothy [*vv* 3, 5], Paul now affectionately reminds his spiritual child [*v* 2] of the prophetic revelation of God's will which had brought him into the ministry. For as Timothy faced the difficult task of preserving the purity of the faith in the church at Ephesus, he was to remember the divine initiative in his calling so that he would be encouraged to rely upon the divine power in fulfilling it. Clearly the reference is to the ministry of Christian prophets, who exercised an important function in the early church, but the gift of inspired prophecy was no longer required after the canon of Scripture was complete. 'Since we no longer have prophets, since we do not have our Lord with us as he was with the disciples, and since we do not have new organs of revelation as in apostolic times, Scripture in its total extent, according to the conception entertained by our Lord and his apostles, is the only revelation of the mind and will of God available to us. This is what the finality of Scripture means for us; it is the only extant revelatory Word of God' (John Murray, 'The Finality and Sufficiency of Scripture', *Collected Writings*, Vol 1, p. 19). In speaking of 'the *prophecies* which led the way to thee', Paul apparently has more than one occasion in view. The commissioning of Paul and Barnabas suggests that there was also a prophecy which led Paul to choose Timothy as his

assistant during the course of the second missionary journey [cf *Acts* 13.1–3; 16.1–3], and this was followed by a
further revelation of the divine will at Timothy's ordination [4.14]. And it is by reliance upon the Word of God
thus given that he is to 'war the good warfare' by defending
the faith against the attacks of the false teachers [*vv* 3–12].

*V*19: **holding faith and a good conscience; which
some having thrust from them made shipwreck concerning the faith:**

As the need for a moral response to the gospel is here
clearly underlined, it is perhaps preferable to take both
references to 'faith' in the subjective sense, though the first
of these would undoubtedly include 'right belief'. Paul's
point is that Timothy must be careful to maintain 'a good
conscience' if he wishes to retain his 'faith' [cf1.5]. This
is precisely where the false teachers went wrong, for when
they violently thrust aside the claims of conscience they
inevitably made shipwreck of their faith. According to the
apostle, the problems of unbelief are not due to certain
intellectual difficulties but to moral failure. And this is
because a bad conscience always brings forth the corrupt
teaching that is congenial to it [*Matt* 7.15–20]. 'The
metaphor of a shipwreck is very apt, for it suggests that
if we wish to reach port with our faith intact, we should
make a good conscience the pilot of our course, or
otherwise there is danger of shipwreck; faith may be sunk
by a bad conscience as by a whirlpool in a stormy sea'
(Calvin).

*V*20: **of whom is Hymenaeus and Alexander; whom**

I delivered unto Satan, that they might be taught not to blaspheme.

Two of the false teachers at Ephesus are cited as examples to be avoided. Another reference to Hymenaeus is found in 2 *Tim* 2.17, 18 (see note there), but nothing further is known of Alexander, who is not to be identified with the two other men of the same name mentioned in *Acts* 19.33 and 2 *Tim* 4.14. By instructing the church to excommunicate these opposers of the truth, Paul delivered them over to the power of Satan [cf *Job* 2.6; 1 *Cor* 5.5]. It is almost certain that this would also involve the supernatural infliction of some form of bodily punishment, but the final clause suggests that its purpose was remedial [*Acts* 13.8–11]. It was hoped that this stern discipline would make them stop reviling God's word and bring them to repentance.

CHAPTER TWO

In keeping with the universal scope of the gospel, Paul urges that prayer is to be made for all men, especially those in authority, so that believers may lead a peaceful and godly life [vv 1, 2]. Such prayer is well-pleasing to God who desires the salvation of all men. For there is but one God and one Mediator, Christ Jesus, who gave himself as a ransom for all, and it was to testify to this that Paul was appointed an apostle to the Gentiles (vv 3–7). With regard to the conduct of worship, he directs that in praying for others men must not be at variance among themselves, while women are to be modest in dress and demeanour [vv 8–10]. Remembering man's priority in creation and her part in the world's sin, a woman ought rather to learn than to teach. But she shall be saved by accepting the rôle of motherhood assigned to her, and by living in faith, love, holiness, and chastity [vv 11–15].

V1: **I exhort therefore, first of all, that supplications, prayers, intercessions, thanksgivings, be made for all men; 2 for kings and all that are in high place; that we may lead a tranquil and quiet life in all godliness and gravity.**

In this section the stress which Paul lays on the word 'all' suggests that he is contrasting the universal scope of the

[37]

gospel with the spirit of Jewish exclusiveness fostered by
the false teachers [*vv* 1–7]. For he 'would naturally be
anxious that the Christian Church should not fail, as the
Jews had done, in recognizing the universality of its
mission' (Lock). Hence his first concern is to underline
the primary importance of praying for all men, especially
for kings and all those in authority, so that peace may be
preserved and piety may flourish unhindered by persecution or strife. A godly life is always the best advertisement
for Christianity, but we are to pray that our witness can
be given in that climate of peace which is most conducive
to the spread of the gospel in the world. 'The supplication
of faithful intercessors for the common weal lays invisible
restraint on the powers of darkness and their tools and
brings reinforcement to honest rulers from the Governor
among the nations (Ps 22.28). Lack of prayer menaces
national as well as individual welfare. Civil government
may be grievously perverted, but divine sanction ratifies
its right to exist' (E. K. Simpson). [cf *Rom* 13.1–7, 1 *Pet*
2.13–17] The apostle enforces the urgency of the duty by
the use of four synonyms: 'supplications' are the requests
which spring from a keenly felt sense of need; 'prayers' is
a general term covering every form of reverent address to
God; 'intercessions' is a word that primarily refers to 'free
familiar prayer, such as boldly draws near to God' (R. C.
Trench), though here it clearly takes on the added meaning
of prayer on behalf of others [cf *Rom* 8.27, 34; *Heb* 7.25];
'thanksgivings' for past mercies must always accompany
our requests for further blessings. Trench points out that
thanksgiving is the one aspect of prayer which will continue in heaven, where it will be larger, deeper, fuller than
here. For only there will the redeemed know how much
they owe to their Lord, 'while all other forms of prayer,

in the very nature of things, will have ceased in the entire
possession and present fruition of the things prayed for'.
[*Rev* 7.12].

*V*3: **This is good and acceptable in the sight of God
our Saviour: 4 who would have all men to be saved,
and come to the knowledge of the truth.**

Such prayer is 'good and acceptable in the sight of God',
who is again called 'our Saviour' (see comment on 1.1).
This is the criterion by which all worship must be tested,
for as Calvin remarks, 'the only genuine rule for right and
proper action is to look to God's good pleasure and to
undertake only what He approves'.

who would have all men to be saved, That God would
have all men to be saved is shown by his provision of a
ransom sufficient for all [*v* 6]. Hence the church may never
hug the gospel to itself, but must always seek to fulfil its
commission to preach the good news to every creature
[*Mark* 16.15]. As God is full of compassion, 'he desires
not the death and destruction of any [*Ezek* 33.11], but the
welfare and salvation of all. Not that he has decreed the
salvation of all, for then all men would be saved; but he
has a good will to the salvation of all, and none perish but
it is their own fault, *Matt* 23.37' (Matthew Henry).

and come to the knowledge of the truth. The ultimate
aim of salvation is to come to the full knowledge of the
truth as this is embodied in Christ [*John* 14.6; *Eph* 4.21].
Consequently the rescue from sin and ignorance must be
followed by 'an advance from this first knowledge of one's
true self as a sinner to the complete and perfect knowledge

[39]

of the truth . . . The word for **full knowledge**, *epignosis*, is repeated four times in these Epistles, 2 *Tim* 2.25; 3.7; *Titus* 1.1, and is contrasted with the knowledge, falsely so called, of the heretical teachers, cf 6.20; *Titus* 1.16' (Humphreys).

V 5: **For there is one God, one mediator also between God and men, *himself* man, Christ Jesus, 6 who gave himself a ransom for all; the testimony *to be borne* in its own times;**

As a further confirmation of the universality of the gospel, Paul cites what seems to be an extract from an early creed, which was probably already current in Ephesus. It crisply sets forth the unity of God, the mediatorial work of Christ, and the universal scope of his vicarious atonement.

For there is one God, This affirms the basic belief of Judaism, which pious Jews recited daily in the *Shema*: 'Hear, O Israel: The Lord our God is one Lord' [*Deut* 6.4]. But what the Jews failed to grasp was that this one God whom they worshipped must also be the God of the Gentiles, and in *Rom* 3.29, 30 Paul refutes Jewish exclusivism by appealing to the unity of God to justify the universal scope of his mission [cf 1 *Cor* 8.6].

one mediator also between God and men, *himself* man, Christ Jesus, With the advent of Christ Job's pathetic cry for an umpire was answered [*Job* 9.32, 33], because he is the one mediator who could bridge the infinite gulf which separated the holy God from sinful men [*John* 14.6]. This unique function belongs to Christ in virtue of the fact that he alone is both God and man.

But while his deity is here assumed, his humanity is emphatically asserted in order to show 'that he belongs to all men without distinction' (A. Oepke, *TDNT*, Vol. IV, p. 619).

who gave himself a ransom for all; This is clearly based on the words of the Lord [*Mark* 10.45], but here the indefinite 'for many' is replaced by the universal 'for all', and instead of the simple noun, we have a rare compound which 'emphasizes the thought of substitution; it is a "substitute-ransom" that is signified' (Leon Morris). God not only desires the salvation of all men [*v* 4], but Christ's finished work is of sufficient value to expiate the sin of all men. 'There are no claims of justice not yet satisfied; there is no sin of man for which an infinite atonement has not been provided. "All things are now ready". Therefore the call to "come" is universal . . . The extent to which a medicine is offered is not limited by the number of persons favourably disposed to buy it and use it. Its adaptation to disease is the sole consideration in selling it, and consequently it is offered to everybody' (W. G. T. Shedd, *Dogmatic Theology*, Vol II, p. 482).

the testimony *to be borne* in its own times; The phrase is too brief for its precise meaning to be clear. It appears to be Paul's own comment on the preceding citation. 'The testimony' probably refers to the witness which the apostle and all future teachers have to give (*v* 7). 'The crowning message of revelation, redemption by the blood of the Lamb, must be published abroad as the supreme panacea for all the ills that flesh is heir to' (Simpson).

V7. **whereunto I was appointed a preacher and an**

apostle (I speak the truth, I lie not), a teacher of the Gentiles in faith and truth.

As a final proof that the church must pray for all men [*vv* 1, 2], Paul appeals to his own appointment by God [1.1] to be a 'herald' (NIV) and an apostle whose distinctive commission made him a teacher of the Gentiles [*Acts* 22.21; *Eph* 3.1ff.]. 'His Epistles therefore should be highly prized by us Gentiles, and diligently studied' (John Trapp). The parenthesis, in which Paul gives the Ephesians a characteristic assurance of his truthfulness (see comment on 1.1), should be connected with what follows as in *Rom* 9.1. For the purpose of this vehement statement is to underline the universality of Paul's mission against the exclusivist ideas of the errorists. The apostle exercised his ministry 'in (the sphere of) faith and truth', which means that he was used by God to bring the Gentiles to 'living faith in the truth of the gospel' (William Hendriksen).

*V*8: **I desire therefore that the men pray in every place, lifting up holy hands, without wrath and disputing.**

In resuming the subject of prayer, Paul next gives directions on how the men are to pray 'in every place', i.e. wherever there is a community of believers [1 *Cor* 1.2; 1 *Thess* 1.8]. The apostle thus makes it plain that in public worship men have the responsibility of leading the congregation in prayer [1 *Cor* 14.34f].

lifting up holy hands, It was the Jewish habit to pray with uplifted hands [1 *Kings* 8.22], and 'the custom passed over into the primitive church, as may be seen from the mural paintings in the catacombs' (Marvin R. Vincent). The adjective 'holy' shows that the outward gesture must be a true expression of the pure intention and devotion of the heart [*Ps* 66.18].

without wrath and disputing. 'Either would mar the charity which prays for all men' (Bernard). With regard to the first, Jeremy Taylor remarked, 'Anger is a perfect alienation of the mind from prayer'; and concerning the second, Bernard notes that 'in our prayers we leave our differences behind us'.

*V*9: **In like manner, that women adorn themselves in modest apparel, with shamefastness and sobriety; not with braided hair, and gold or pearls or costly raiment; 10 but (which becometh women professing godliness) through good works.**

'In like manner' indicates that Paul is still speaking about the conduct of public worship, but the relevance of his remarks on the dress and deportment of women also extends to the effect of their behaviour upon society, since 'good works' are the 'fitting ornament' of women who make a profession of 'godliness' [5.10; cf 1 *Pet* 3.1–6]. As ostentation and extravagance in dress hardly point to a mind set on heavenly things [*Col* 3.2], Christian women are to dress modestly, 'with decency and propriety' (NIV). 'The outward modesty which makes itself known in the dress, is to be accompanied by inward purity and chastity, since the former would otherwise be of no account' (Huther). Obviously, the practical application of the principle here set forth will always be expressed in a manner that is considered appropriate to the cultural and social climate of the time. What is important is to remember the unchanging principle: 'Let all things be done decently and in order' [1 *Cor* 14.40].

*V*11: **Let a woman learn in quietness with all subjection. 12 But I permit not a woman to teach, nor to have dominion over a man, but to be in quietness.**

Although Paul elsewhere shows that women have equal standing with men in Christ [*Gal* 3.28], he also insists that fellowship in Christ does not remove the natural distinction between the sexes, which was established by the priority given to man in creation [*v* 13]. Paul will not permit a woman to assume the place of leadership in the church as an authoritative teacher of doctrine, because that would set aside the order of nature and put her in the position of exercising authority over the men in the congregation. 'Paul refers to teaching *Scripture* and not to imparting intellectual secular information to the mind. The public teacher of God's people does not only tell others what they need to know, but in the capacity of such a teacher he stands before his audience to rule and govern it with the Word . . . No woman may step into the place of the man without violating the very Word she would try to teach to both women and men. Her effort to do so would be self-contradictory in God's eyes despite what the world may say' (Lenski). Since the prohibition only applies to the conduct of public worship, a woman can teach other women [*Titus* 2.3, 4], take a Sunday school class, and instruct her own children [*Titus* 1.5; 3.14, 15]. But when in church, she is to learn in silence, and must not try to usurp the teaching function which is denied to her by the Word of God.

[44]

V 13: **For Adam was first formed, then Eve; 14 and Adam was not beguiled, but the woman being beguiled hath fallen into transgression:**

Paul gives two reasons for this ban. First, he appeals to the fact that Adam was created before Eve [*Gen* 2.21ff.], and in the light of 1 *Cor* 11.8f. ('the man is not of the woman, but the woman of the man: for neither was the man created for the woman; but the woman for the man'), this means that 'the origin and *raison d'être* of woman are to be found in man' (H. Schlier, *TDNT*, Vol III, p. 679). As therefore God's purpose in creating Eve was to provide a 'help meet' for Adam [*Gen* 2.20], it is unlawful for a woman to take to herself the headship which belongs to man.

Secondly, Paul shows that Eve's part in the Fall was due to her being deceived [2 *Cor* 11.3]. 'The Serpent deceived the woman; the woman did not deceive the man, but persuaded him: *Gen* 3.17, *thou hast hearkened to the voice of thy wife* . . . In the preceding verse [*v* 13], we are taught why the woman should not *exercise authority*, now, why she should not *teach*; more easily deceived, she more easily deceives' (J. A. Bengel). Paul puts all the emphasis on the word 'deceive' (mentioned twice), in order to drive home this particular lesson. He is not blaming Eve to excuse Adam, for he shows in Rom 5.12ff. that the whole race was ruined by the transgression of the *one man* who was its Head.

V 15: **but she shall be saved through her childbearing, if they continue in faith and love and sanctification with sobriety.**

Instead of hankering after the teaching office which does

not belong to her (*v* 11), let the woman gratefully receive the divinely ordained rôle of motherhood [5.14; *Titus* 2.4, 5], notwithstanding the unnatural prohibition of marriage advocated by the false teachers [4.3]. Of course Paul is not saying that she will win salvation 'through' or by means of childbirth. The preposition used here is the *dia* of accompanying circumstances, and the assurance thus conveyed is that she shall be saved 'in' her child-bearing. It is by accepting her proper sphere that she fulfils her true destiny. This is the plain meaning of the words. To take 'the childbearing' as a veiled reference to the Incarnation is fanciful, to say the least!

if they continue in faith and love and sanctification with sobriety. Paul has been either speaking of women in the plural or of woman in a generic sense from verse 9, and so the sudden transition to the plural 'they' should occasion no surprise. To bear and rear children is indeed a 'good work' [*v* 10], but women are not saved in a manner that is different from men. As they are saved the moment they believe, so they must continue in faith and the state of grace ('love and sanctification with sobriety' or chastity) if they are to attain the promised consummation [cf *Col* 1.23].

CHAPTER THREE

Paul here specifies the qualifications required of those who aspire to leadership in the church. A bishop or overseer must be above reproach, not a recent convert, but a man who is able to teach, and whose well-ordered family life provides an example to the church and commands the respect of the community at large (vv 1–7). The same high moral standards must also be evident in those who are chosen to serve as deacons and deaconesses (vv 8–13). He hopes to visit Timothy soon, but meanwhile stresses the importance of observing these directions, since they outline the conduct that is proper to the church. Anyone who is tempted to belittle the church by a careless walk is reminded that it is nothing less than God's household, the very pillar and bulwark of the truth. Paul now cites part of a hymn to show that the secret of godliness was revealed through the One whom all believers worship as their Incarnate and Glorified Lord [vv 14–16].

V 1: **Faithful is the saying, If a man seeketh the office of a bishop, he desireth a good work.**

Faithful is the saying, The second of the 'faithful sayings' omits the words 'and worthy of all acceptation' [1.15; 4.9], because its application is limited to a particular group. Its purpose is not to proclaim the message of the gospel, but to commend the ministry of the gospel [2 *Tim* 2.2]. 'The particular response which is in view is the encouragement of those who should seek the good work of serving as a bishop' (George W. Knight, *The Faithful Sayings in the Pastoral Epistles*, p. 144).

If a man seeketh the office of a bishop, In the apostolic church the two terms 'elder' and 'bishop' were used interchangeably to designate the same person [*Titus* 1.5–7]. 'The term "elder" indicates the mature spiritual experience and understanding of those so described; the term "bishop", or "overseer", indicates the character of the work undertaken' (W. E. Vine). [*Acts* 20.28; 1 *Pet* 5.2,3.] It is evident that the kind of seeking here intended is 'not the prompting of a carnal ambition, but the aspiration of a heart which has itself experienced the grace of God, and which longs to see others coming to participate in the heavenly gift' (Fairbairn).

he desireth a good work. 'It is a work, a business, not ease; *Acts* 15.38; *Phil* 2.30' (Bengel). In the following verses it is made clear that such a work can only be accomplished by men of good character [*vv* 2–7].

*V*2: **The bishop therefore must be without reproach, the husband of one wife, temperate, sober-minded, orderly, given to hospitality, apt to teach;**

In the fifteen qualifications which follow, Paul stresses that the man who aspires to the ministry must be an example to the flock. The first seven describe the virtues with which he must be endowed [*v* 2], the next seven indicate the vices from which he must be exempt and outline his conduct in regard to his family and the church [*vv* 3–6], while the last relates to his reputation in the world outside [*v* 7].

without reproach, The list begins with the general qualification of blamelessness. The word used literally means 'not to be laid hold of', and so not open to just censure. 'Every faithful pastor must be such as against whom no just exception can be laid, no gross fault objected. Involuntary failings and unavoidable infirmities have a pardon, of course, both with God and all good men' (Trapp).

the husband of but one wife, (NIV). The same high moral standard is required of deacons [*v* 12]. It does not mean that a single man cannot serve or that an overseer cannot marry again following the death of his first wife [*Rom* 7.1–3]. 'The emphasis is on *one* wife's husband, and the sense is that he have nothing to do with any other woman. He must be a man who cannot be taken hold of on the score of sexual promiscuity or laxity' (Lenski).

temperate, self-controlled, respectable, (NIV) As to his personal qualities, he must be a man who is not given to any kind of excess, whose well-disciplined mind finds its natural expression in a well-ordered respectable life.

given to hospitality, This word literally means 'loving strangers'. In a day when inns were dens of extortion and vice, there was a great need to provide safe lodging for Christian travellers and for those made fugitives by persecution [*Rom* 12.13; *Heb* 13.2; 1 *Pet* 4.9].

[49]

apt to teach; It is only here and in verse 5 that Paul touches on the actual work of an overseer. As well as possessing a sound knowledge of the faith, he must have the ability to teach it to others [2 *Tim* 2.2; *Titus* 1.9]. 'What is required here is not merely a voluble tongue, for we see many whose easy fluency contains nothing that can edify. Paul is rather commending wisdom in knowing how to apply God's Word to the profit of His people' (Calvin).

*V*3: **no brawler, no striker; but gentle, not contentious, no lover of money;**

Of the next five on the list, the one positive virtue required is sandwiched between four negatives. 'No brawler' is no improvement on the AV's 'not given to wine' (cf NIV). The word signifies 'a common tippler, whether he drinks to the loss of his reason or no; a wine-bibber, that makes bibbing at a tavern his trade: no sitter at wine' (Poole). In his conduct toward others, the overseer must be 'no striker' either with tongue or hand [2 *Cor* 11.20], but is to be of a 'gentle' and forbearing spirit. As befits a minister of the new covenant, he will not be a man who is always insisting upon his '*legal* rights, lest they should be pushed into *moral* wrongs' (R. C. Trench). 'Not contentious' shows that the herald of God's peace must not stir up strife with quarrelsome words. The usefulness of many a ministry has been destroyed by a failure to radiate the peace which was only proclaimed from the pulpit and not shown in the life. Finally, the one who directs others to heaven must not be 'a lover of money' [6.9–11; *Matt* 6.19–21]. This is a needful word of warning, for the earth-bound desires of a covetous spirit always clip the wings of faith and love.

*V*4: **one that ruleth well his own house, having** *his* **children in subjection with all gravity; 5 (but if a man knoweth not how to rule his own house, how shall he take care of the church of God?)**

In contrast to the unscriptural demand of the Roman Catholic Church for a celibate priesthood [4.3], Paul takes it for granted that the overseer will be a married man with a family, because 'those who know ordinary life and are well practised in the duties that human relationships impose, are far better trained and fitted to rule in the Church' (Calvin). Thus the good pastor will be a man whose 'gravity' or calm dignity will secure the respect and ready obedience of his children. Paul's rhetorical question argues from the lesser to the greater. For if a man is unable to govern his own family, he is clearly not fitted for the more difficult task of caring for the church of God, 'which is a larger society, with all the members of which he is not so constantly present, and over whom he hath not such a coercive power, and as to whom a far greater care must be taken' (Poole).

*V*6: **not a novice, lest being puffed up he fall into the condemnation of the devil.**

In his directions to Timothy, Paul insists that the overseer must not be a 'novice', a 'newly planted' convert, or he may become blinded by 'a smoke-screen of pride' (A. T. Robertson) and 'fall under the same judgment as the devil' (NIV). As pride was the cause of the devil's downfall, those in high places of spiritual responsibility must take care to keep low before God [*Is* 14.12–15; *Luke* 10.17,18; 2 *Pet* 2.4; *Jude* 6]. The absence of this directive from the parallel passage in Titus is an indication that church organization in Crete was in a very much less advanced state than in Ephesus. In the case of newly formed churches, the apostles had to appoint converts to this office, 'because no others were available; and men appointed in such circumstances would have no temptation to be puffed up any more than would the leaders of a forlorn hope' (White). But the situation was quite different in a well-established church where the elevation of a novice to a position of prestige might fill him with pride and cause him to fall.

V 7: **Moreover he must have good testimony from them that are without; lest he fall into reproach and the snare of the devil.**

The final qualification laid down by Paul for the overseer of the local church is that he must have 'a good reputation with outsiders' (NIV). It is true that unbelievers have no right to interfere with the affairs of the church, but because they have the law of God written in their hearts [*Rom* 2,15], their moral judgments are regarded by Paul as being worthy of respect. 'There is something blameworthy in a man's character if the consensus of outside opinion be unfavourable to him; no matter how much he may be admired and respected by his own party' (White). To appoint a man of doubtful reputation to a place of leadership in the Christian community would expose him to the reproach of men and 'the snare of the devil', who is here represented as the great hunter of souls [cf 6.9; 2 *Tim* 2.26]. The idea is that 'the disgrace incurred by the one who has not a good testimony from the non-Christians, is used by the devil as a snare, not only to tempt him, but also to seduce him into apostasy from the gospel' (Huther).

*V*8: **Deacons in like manner** *must be* **grave, not double-tongued, not given to much wine, not greedy of filthy lucre;** 9 **holding the mystery of the faith in a pure conscience.**

Although the Seven appointed to serve in Acts 6 are not actually called 'deacons', it seems reasonable to assume from the practical duties assigned to them that they were the forerunners of those who were later given this title [*Phil* 1.1]. 'The qualifications looked for in deacons stress sound character and a firm hold on the true faith. There is no mention of capacity for teaching or the like. It may perhaps be inferred that the primary tasks of the deacons were administrative and financial. The scriptural references seem to make it clear that the diaconate formed one of the two recognized orders constituting the local ministry of the Christian Church' (Leon Morris, *Ministers of God*, p. 90). Deacons must also be men of serious character and dignified bearing; not saying one thing to one man and something different to the next, as did Bunyan's parson Mr. Two-tongues; not addicted to wine; and not out for dishonest gain. With regard to the last, Charles R. Erdman remarks, 'Judas was not the last treasurer who betrayed his Lord for a few pieces of silver'.

holding the mystery of the faith in a pure conscience.
'The mystery of the faith' is the revelation given in Christ of the once hidden purpose of God [*v* 16; *Rom* 16.25, 26]. But the accent here falls on the ethical demand for a pure conscience [1.5; 1.19]. 'It is as if the pure conscience were

[53]

the vessel in which the mystery of the faith is preserved'
(B. Weiss).

*V*10: **And let these also first be proved; then let them
serve as deacons, if they be blameless.**

'Also' indicates that deacons no less than overseers must
be men of blameless (or 'unaccused') character [*vv* 2–7].
Let them 'first be proved' does not refer to a formal
examination or a period of probation, but clearly has in
view the general verdict of the local church concerning
their life and conversation [*Acts* 6.3].

*V*11: **Women in like manner *must be* grave, not slanderers, temperate, faithful in all things.**

It would be strange if Paul singled out deacons' wives for
special mention when the wife of the overseer held a much
more influential position in the church, and it is preferable
to understand the repetition of 'in like manner' [*v* 8] as
making another group and thus introducing the qualifications required of women who serve as deacons. They
too must be dignified, not retailers of 'devilish' gossip
('slanderers' is literally 'devils'), but temperate and reliable
in everything. Their duties included assisting at the baptism of women, pastoral work among the sick and poor,
and carrying official messages [*Rom* 16.1, 2]. 'Thus while
the New Testament prohibits women from assuming the
rôle of leadership in the church [2.11–12; 1 *Cor* 14.34],
they do appear as having a significant ministry in the
church along with men in the subordinate auxiliary rôle
of the diaconate' (Robert L. Saucy).

*V*12: **Let deacons be husbands of one wife, ruling** *their* **children and their own houses well.** 13 **For they that have served well as deacons gain to themselves a good standing, and great boldness in the faith which is in Christ Jesus.**

In reverting to the male diaconate, Paul requires them to maintain the same high standard of family life as that laid down for the overseer (see comment on *vv* 2, 4–5). Those who serve faithfully in this subordinate office 'gain to themselves a good standing' among their fellow-believers and in the community at large, and this consciousness of their personal integrity also gives them 'great boldness in the faith which is in Christ Jesus'. But such boldness 'is only truly safe and humble if it moves in an atmosphere of faith in the protecting and strengthening presence of Christ Jesus. Here the dominant quality and requisite of all Christian service, personal faith in Christ Jesus, is recalled' (Parry).

*V*14: **These things write I unto thee, hoping to come unto thee shortly;** 15 **but if I tarry long, that thou mayest know how men ought to behave themselves in the house of God, which is the church of the living God, the pillar and ground of the truth.**

In disclosing his purpose in writing to Timothy, Paul enables us to grasp the inner meaning of the Pastoral Epistles, for the passage forms the bridge between the preceding regulations about the ministry and the onslaught against false teaching which follows. The abiding significance of the lesson thus taught by the apostle is that unless the church is careful to maintain a faithful ministry it will be impossible to preserve the purity of its faith in Christ [*v* 16]. Paul here sets forth the dignity of the church in a threefold description that is designed to underline the kind of conduct which reverence for God demands. First, we must realize that the church is not simply a voluntary association of men, but the very dwelling-place of God. 'There are good reasons why God should call the Church His House, for not only has He received us as His sons by the grace of adoption, but He Himself dwells in the midst of us' (Calvin). Secondly, in contrast to the folly of worshipping dumb idols, the life of the believing community is derived from, and determined by, the inspiring and directing presence of 'the living God' [2 *Cor* 3.3; 1 *Thess* 1.9; *Heb* 12.22]. Finally, the church is the very 'pillar and bulwark of the truth' (RSV). As the recipient of God's truth, the church is committed to uphold and defend it against the attacks of those whose teaching emanates from the father of lies [4.1f]. As Fairbairn well says, 'The truth is not of the church's making, but of God's revealing: she has it, not as of her own, but from above; and has it not to alter or modify at her own will, but to keep as a sacred treasure for the glory of God and the good of men . . . Rightly understood, therefore, this passage determines nothing for Rome, or for any church which rests its claim to apostolicity on historical descent. The grand test is, does she hold by the truth of God? Is she in her belief and practice a witness for this? Or does she gainsay and pervert it?' [2 *Tim* 3.16f].

V 16: **And without controversy great is the mystery of godliness;**

> **He who was manifested in the flesh,**
> **Justified in the spirit,**

Seen of angels,
Preached among the nations,
Believed on in the world,
Received up in glory.

It is generally agreed that Paul here quotes a fragment of
an early Christian hymn. The six lines fall naturally into
three contrasting pairs: (1) flesh-spirit, (2) angels-nations,
(3) world-glory. 'The movement of thought is spatial
rather than chronological because the important point is
that the Saviour has reunited heaven and earth' (Robert H.
Gundry, 'The Form, Meaning and Background of the
Hymn Quoted in 1 *Timothy* 3.16' in *Apostolic History and
the Gospel*, p. 207).

And confessedly great is the mystery of piety; All
believers unite in confessing the supreme importance of
the mystery which God has revealed in the gospel, for
they know that the secret of true piety is nothing less than
Christ himself [cf *Col* 1.27]. 'And a "mystery of godliness" the gospel is called, because, being believed, it
transformeth men into the same image, and stirs up in
them admirable affections of piety' (Trapp).

**He who was manifested in the flesh/Justified in the
spirit** Although the quotation is abruptly introduced with
the pronoun 'who', none of Paul's readers 'would hesitate
to supply the subject, Jesus Christ' (B. B. Warfield). In
this couplet the contrast is not between the humanity and
divinity of Christ, but between two successive stages of
his life. The preincarnate Son 'was manifested in the flesh'
during the period of his humiliation, but he was justified
in the realm of the Spirit when by his resurrection he

entered into the state of exaltation. As Christ died under the cloud of our guilt [2 *Cor* 5.21], we could not be justified until the resurrection of our Surety removed this verdict of condemnation and effectively affirmed the representative character of his perfect righteousness [*Rom* 4.25]. 'Christ's resurrection was the *de facto* declaration of God in regard to his being just. His quickening bears in itself the testimony of his justification. God, through suspending the forces of death operating on Him, declared that the ultimate, the supreme consequence of sin had reached its termination. In other words, resurrection had annulled the sentence of condemnation' (G. Vos as cited by Richard B. Gaffin, to whom I am indebted for the substance of this comment).

Seen of angels/Preached among the nations Since the hymn celebrates the triumph of Christ incarnate, 'seen of angels' probably refers to the worship accorded by the angelic host to Christ at his ascension [*Phil* 2.9f.], and this would fit in with the final line, 'received up in glory'. 'Preached among the nations' shows that the early church was eager to fulfil its missionary mandate to preach the gospel to every creature, and the hymn's stress on the universal scope of the gospel leads Robert Gundry to make the interesting suggestion that it may have originated in Syrian Antioch, the church which sent forth Paul and Barnabas to evangelize the Gentiles [*Acts* 11.19–26; 13.1ff.]. As Bernard notes, The revelation to Gentiles is *mediate*, by preaching, while 'the revelation to the higher orders or created intelligences is *immediate*, by vision'.

Believed on in the world/Received up in glory The final couplet sets forth the consummation of Christ's saving work on earth and in heaven. 'Believed on in the world' points to the amazing result of the universal preaching of the good news [Col 1.23]; 'received up in glory' means that Christ was taken up to the realm of glory and there enthroned in the seat of all authority and power.

CHAPTER FOUR

Through the Spirit the apostle warns Timothy of the rise of deceitful teachers, who will enforce ascetic practices in violation of the declared will of God [vv 1–5]. Timothy can best combat such errors by teaching the true faith, avoiding unprofitable speculations, and providing an example of godly living. He must be diligent in fulfilling his ministry and developing his gift, so that his progress may be seen by all. For in thus taking heed to himself and his doctrine, he will save both himself and his hearers [vv 6–16].

*V*1: **But the Spirit saith expressly, that in later times some shall fall away from the faith, giving heed to seducing spirits and doctrines of demons,**

Since Paul places all the emphasis on the Spirit as the divine author of the prediction, we cannot be certain that the apostle was the recipient of this revelation, but it is not improbable in view of his previous warning to the same church [*Acts* 20.29, 30]. 'In later times' does not refer to the remote future (as in 'the last days' of 2 *Tim* 3.1), but to an impending crisis of which the first signs are already present [*vv* 3–5]. The apostasy of 'some' from their profession of 'the faith' will be due to their paying attention to deceiving spirits and the doctrines taught by demons. Engaged as he was in a spiritual conflict, Paul knew very well that his wrestling was not against flesh and blood, but against the malevolent powers of darkness [*Eph* 6.12]. 'They are the *ultimate*, the false teachers of the next verse being the *proximate*, cause of the errors about to appear in the Church' (Bernard).

*V*2: **through the hypocrisy of men that speak lies, branded in their own conscience as with a hot iron;**

through the specious falsehoods of men whose own conscience is branded with the devil's sign. (NEB) Since the false teachers are engaged in the devil's work, their conscience is branded with the sign which indicates his ownership. The metaphor is taken from the practice of branding slaves and criminals. 'The meaning is that they are in bondage to secret sin. Proclaiming a doctrine which makes strong ascetic demands, they are themselves controlled by self-seeking and covetousness. They are secretly the slaves of satanic and demonic powers which make them their instruments' (J. Schneider, *TDNT*, Vol III, p. 644).

*V*3: **forbidding to marry, *and commanding* to abstain from meats, which God created to be received with thanksgiving by them that believe and know the truth.**

Paul here shows that the spurious spirituality which pretends to attain a higher perfection by abstaining from outward things is an impeachment of the wisdom of God in creation [*Gen* 1.31]. Having already endorsed the divine ordinance of marriage [2.15; 3.2,12], the apostle condemns the devilish demand for celibacy by implication rather than by argument, but elsewhere he clearly teaches that the unlawful requirements of asceticism can never be the means of promoting a superior state of sanctity [cf *Col* 2.20–23]. With regard to the prohibition of certain foods, Paul insists that such a ban is contrary to the will of God, who created these gifts 'to be received with thanksgiving by them that believe and know the truth'. Ignorance, far from being the mother of devotion, keeps its votaries in bondage to the superstition which prevents them from receiving God's blessings with gratitude. In contrast to the unbelieving Jews or to the half-instructed 'weak brethren' [*Rom* 14.21], believers who fully know the truth have no scruples in freely partaking of that bounty which they thankfully acknowledge to be the fruit of God's covenant love.

V4: For every creature of God is good, and nothing is to be rejected, if it be received with thanksgiving: 5 for it is sanctified through the word of God and prayer, .

'For' introduces the reason for the whole of the preceding statement [*v* 3]. Because the goodness of God is manifested in creation, every creature he made is good, and therefore nothing is to be rejected or thrown away, provided it is received with thanksgiving [*Gen* 1.31; *Mark* 7.15; *Acts* 10.15]. As if to anticipate the objection that some foods were expressly forbidden by the Mosaic Law, Paul repeats the condition of blessing to show that '*thanksgiving* disannuls the Law in each particular case. Nothing over which thanksgiving can be pronounced is any longer included in the category of things tabooed' (White). For the food is thus 'sanctified through the word of God and prayer'. 'It becomes holy to the eater; not that it was unclean in itself, but that his scruples or thanklessness might make it so to him' (Lock). In this clear reference to grace before meals [*Mark* 6.41; 14.22; *Acts* 27.35], the word of God and prayer are joined together, because we speak to God on the basis of his word and use expressions which are taken from it. The early examples of such prayers which have come down to us are 'packed with Scriptural phrases' (Bernard).

V 6: **If thou put the brethren in mind of these things, thou shalt be a good minister of Christ Jesus, nourished in the words of the faith, and of the good doctrine which thou hast followed** *until now*:

By submitting these truths to the brethren [*vv* 4, 5], Timothy will fortify them against error [*vv* 1–3], and prove himself a good minister of Christ Jesus. Although some prefer the praise of men, a godly pastor would rather choose 'to be accounted a good servant of Christ, so that during the whole of his ministry this should be his only aim' (Calvin). Timothy will attain this goal by continuing to be nourished by 'the words of the faith and of the good doctrine' – for it is loyal adherence to the objective truth of the gospel that makes a good minister – and this is the course he has followed until now. 'Many who have purely learned Christ from their boyhood afterwards fall away with the passing of time, but Paul says that Timothy was not one of them' (Calvin). [2 *Tim* 3.14, 15]

V 7: **but refuse profane and old wives' fables. And exercise thyself unto godliness:**

[63]

In sharp contrast to 'the good doctrine', Timothy must have nothing to do with those unholy myths which resemble the tall stories told by credulous old women! [1.4; *Titus* 1.14] 'The *myths* with which the heretics offer supposed religious truths are profane. They have nothing to do with God and lead astray from Him. It can hardly be said more plainly that the *myths* and NT religion are mutually exclusive' (G. Stählin, *TDNT*, Vol IV, p. 787). Instead of giving heed to such folly, Timothy is to train himself for a life of godliness. As true godliness is rooted in Christ's saving work, it is fundamentally the *gift* of God's grace [*Titus* 2.11, 12]. But it is also a *demand* in that our growth in grace calls for an obedience to God's will which requires strenuous self-discipline [*vv* 8,10; 6.11, 12].

*V*8: **for bodily exercise is profitable for a little; but godliness is profitable for all things, having promise of the life which now is, and of that which is to come. 9 Faithful is the saying, and worthy of all acceptation.**

Most commentators are agreed that the formula of verse 9 refers back to verse 8, because this is more like a proverbial saying than verse 10, which rather appeals to Christian experience to confirm its truth ('for'). The third of the 'faithful sayings' contrasts the limited value of gymnastic exercise ('profitable for *a little*') with the absolute value of godliness ('profitable for *all things*'). The far greater superiority of godliness consists in its 'having promise of the life which now is, and of that which is to come'. Godliness is profitable, not because it offers a guarantee of worldly prosperity [6.5ff], but because it carries with it a promise of that everlasting life 'in which we already participate in the period of Christ, and to which we look forward in fulness then' (G. Stählin, *TDNT*, Vol IV, p. 1120). As God is the giver of this new life in Christ [2 *Tim* 1.1], he remains the object of hope [*Titus* 1.2], so that even present struggles can be regarded as a preparation for future glory [*v* 10]. Thus 'the distinction is not between two kinds of life, but the two conditions under which the one life is lived' (Parry).

V 10: **For to this end we labour and strive, because we have our hope set on the living God, who is the Saviour of all men, specially of them that believe.**

The experience of Paul and his fellow-labourers is a standing testimony to the truth of the saying [*v* 8]: For with this end in view they toil and struggle [*Col* 1.29], because they have fixed their hope on God (the) *living*, who is 'therefore able to give life now and hereafter' (Lock). The further description of God as 'the Saviour of *all* men' is evidently directed against the rigorous demands of the false teachers, and is intended to show that God is not merely the Saviour of a handful of ascetics [*vv* 3, 4]. For God's offer of salvation applies to all men without distinction [2.4], and this calls for the universal proclamation of his word of grace in order to bring the lost to faith [*Titus* 1.3]. But to reassure any Christians who were disturbed by the exclusive claims of the heretics, Paul adds that God is *especially* the Saviour of believers because the expectations of those whose hope is placed in the living God can never be disappointed. It is a mistake to detach this verse from its 'life-situation' and make it either a prop for universalism or the enemy of predestination. We shall be able to avoid such errors only as we seek to interpret every text within its particular context.

V11: **These things command and teach.**

In case Timothy had any misgivings about his task in Ephesus, Paul encourages him to leave his hearers in no doubt of his authority. Although teaching precedes commanding in point of time, 'command' is here placed before 'teach' because the church had to be recalled to certain fundamental truths which were in danger of being forgotten ('these things' = *vv* 6–10). 'Teach the tractable, command the obstinate, lay God's charge upon all' (Trapp).

V12: **Let no man despise thy youth; but be thou an ensample to them that believe, in word, in manner of life, in love, in faith, in purity.**

Timothy was relatively youthful for the heavy responsibility of acting as the apostle's representative in Ephesus, even though he was probably between 35 and 40 years of age. Hence his character and conduct must be such as to give none any occasion to despise his lack of years. No doubt the exhortation was also intended to have a salutary effect on the Ephesian congregation, 'for no Greek maxim was more familiar than the subordination of youth to age' (E. K. Simpson). So if he is to command respect, Timothy must be an 'ensample' to believers, i.e. 'not merely an example *to* them but a model *for* them' (Bernard). [cf *Titus* 2.7f] Paul indicates five spheres in which this pattern is to be made distinct. As to outward conduct, both speech and conduct must be above reproach, and with respect to inward disposition, it should be clear that this has been shaped by the three essential graces of love, faith, and purity.

V 13: **Till I come, give heed to reading, to exhortation, to teaching.**

Paul has already indicated that he hopes soon to visit Ephesus [3.14], and meanwhile Timothy is to devote himself to the work of the ministry. Three aspects of this work are singled out for special mention. First, there is the public reading of the Scripture, a practice taken over from the synagogue [*Luke* 4.16, 17; *Acts* 15.21; *2 Cor* 3.14]. Apostolic letters were also read to the congregation, and we see in this tacit recognition of their inspiration and authority the origin of the New Testament canon [*Col* 4.16; *1 Thess* 5.27; *2 Pet* 3.15, 16; *Rev* 1.3]. Next came the exhortation or sermon that followed the reading and was based upon it. This was also an adoption of what was the custom in the synagogue [*Acts* 13.15]. Finally, there is the teaching or catechetical instruction, which served to explain the doctrines of the faith to new converts and provided them with the guidelines for Christian living [cf *Rom* 12.7; *Titus* 2.1–14].

V 14: **Neglect not the gift that is in thee, which was given thee by prophecy, with the laying on of the hands of the presbytery.**

In urging Timothy not to neglect the gift that is in him, Paul is not implying that he is failing in his duty, since the negative simply expresses what is positively required: 'Always be giving this your diligent attention!' But the exhortation is necessary because 'the gift' is not a magical

[67]

endowment which works without the co-operation of its recipient; 'it may be neglected and needs to be kindled into a flame (see 2 *Tim* 1.6). To neglect God's gifts, whether of nature or of grace, is a sin' (Bernard). The gift which is in view is that which fitted Timothy for the work of the ministry. Paul's choice of Timothy at Lystra was confirmed by prophetic utterances [1.18; *Acts* 16.1–3], and the impartation of the gift was recognized in connection with the symbolic laying on of hands by the elders in which Paul also joined [2 *Tim* 1.6; cf *Acts* 13.1–3]. 'The essence of the matter does not lie in the particular official hands that ministered in Timothy's ordination; but the grace was God's immediate and inward bestowment, attested by the voice of His Spirit in the Church, then sealed and acknowledged on the Church's part in the appropriate form' (Findlay).

V 15: **Be diligent in these things; give thyself wholly to them; that thy progress may be manifest unto all.**

After reminding Timothy of the gift which qualified him for the task, Paul now bids him to be diligent in the exercise of his ministry [*vv* 12–14]. He must be so absorbed in these duties that his 'progress' (a word often used of progress in philosophy by Stoic writers) may be evident to all. Two points are significant here: 1. that the true spiritual progress of the Christian is visible to others as well as himself, and 2. that although in the pastoral exhortation of this section *progress* seems to be a matter of human effort, 'in the last resort, as the development of a grace, it is like all genuine NT *progress* a gift of God' (G. Stählin, *TDNT*, Vol. VI, p. 714).

*V*16: **Take heed to thyself, and to thy teaching. Continue in these things; for in doing this thou shalt save both thyself and them that hear thee.**

Paul concludes with a double charge: 1. Timothy must take heed to himself, for the minister must be the first to profit from the truth which he presses upon his hearers [2 *Tim* 2.6], lest having preached to others he should find himself rejected [1 *Cor* 9.27]; 2. He must take heed to his own presentation of the truth, for those under his care must not only be instructed in 'the doctrine', but also have their particular needs met with the right word at the right time [*Prov* 15.23]. This is followed by the assurance that if Timothy perseveres in 'these things' (i.e. all the preceding injunctions which were summed up in *v* 15) he shall save both himself and those who hear him. 'Save' here means full and final salvation. 'Nor should it seem strange that Paul ascribes to Timothy the work of saving the Church, for all that are won for God are saved and it is by the preaching of the Gospel that we are gathered to Christ. And just as the unfaithfulness ·or negligence of a pastor is fatal to the Church, so it is right for its salvation to be ascribed to his faithfulness and diligence. It is indeed true that it is God alone who saves and not even the smallest part of His glory can rightly be transferred to men. But God's glory is is no way diminished by His using the labour of men in bestowing salvation' (Calvin). [*Eph* 4.11].

CHAPTER FIVE

With regard to church discipline, Paul first shows that Timothy's admonitions must be suited to the age and sex of the persons addressed [vv 1, 2]. In dealing with widows, it is necessary to distinguish between those in need of the church's support and those with relatives who are well able to take care of them [vv 3–8]. No widow under the age of sixty may be enrolled unless she is known to be of good character, and younger widows should be encouraged to marry again and bring up a family [vv 11–16]. Elders are to be honoured and rewarded for their work; no accusation should be received against an elder without proof, but those found guilty of an offence must be openly reproved that the rest may fear to imitate them [vv 17–21]. Timothy is charged to act without prejudice, cautioned against ordaining any man in haste, and bidden to shun all that is evil [vv 21, 22]. After advising Timothy to take a little wine for the sake of his health, Paul reverts to the need for discernment in judging character because outward appearances can be very deceptive [vv 23–25].

V 1: **Rebuke not an elder, but exhort him as a father; the younger men as brethren: 2 the elder women as mothers; the younger as sisters, in all purity.**

In fulfilling the pastoral office Timothy must show church members the same respect he would give to his own family. An older man (the word here does not refer to an 'elder' of the church, cf *v* 17) should not be harshly rebuked, but entreated as a father. Although the others named are also governed by the verb 'exhort', it is possible that Paul passes from the idea of admonition to Timothy's general relations with the various groups in his flock (J. N. D. Kelly). He must treat younger men as brothers, the elder women as mothers, and the younger women as sisters. In the latter case he adds the cautionary clause, 'in all purity', since nothing 'will so easily make or mar the young preacher as his conduct with young women' (A. T. Robertson).

*V*3: **Honour widows that are widows indeed.**

As the duty of supporting widows was recognized by the church from the beginning [*Acts* 6.1], it is not surprising to find Paul endorsing this practice. But at the outset of his discussion he lays down the important qualification: 'Honour widows that are widows *indeed*', i.e. those who are truly bereft, having neither husband nor kinsfolk to support them [*v* 4]. In contrast to the common disparagement of widows, the word 'honour' recalls the fifth commandment [*Exod* 20.12], and thus shows that they are not only entitled to respect but to material provision as well [*Matt* 15.4ff].

*V*4: **But if any widow hath children or grandchildren, let them learn first to show piety towards their own family, and to requite their parents: for this is acceptable in the sight of God.**

But if a widow has a family, the responsibility for her

support rests with them and not the church. Let her relatives learn that their first duty is to practise piety towards their own family, and 'make a return to those who brought them up' (Arndt-Gingrich). A ready fulfilment of this natural obligation is not only reasonable, but is also approved of God because it is in accordance with his revealed will [*Exod* 20.12].

*V*5: **Now she that is a widow indeed, and desolate, hath her hope set on God, and continueth in supplications and prayers night and day.**

This gives the characteristics of the true widow who is eligible to receive the support of the church. Having been left entirely alone, she has fixed her hope on God, the Guardian of widows, and like Anna is given to constant prayer [*Luke* 2.37]. The expression 'night and day' is 'indicative of the *when* rather than the *how long*; not *throughout* night and day, but *by* night as well as *by* day – a steady and regular habit of devotion' (Fairbairn). [cf 1 *Thess* 3.10].

*V*6: **But she that giveth herself to pleasure is dead while she liveth.**

By contrast the widow who only lives for pleasure is spiritually dead even while she lives, and has no claim on the church's charity [cf *Rev* 3.1]. 'Life in worldly pleasure is only life in appearance' (H. J. Holtzmann).

*V*7: **These things also command, that they may be without reproach.**

Timothy must take care that Paul's instructions concerning widows are obeyed, for to maintain a credible witness it is necessary to ensure that those supported by the church, whether bishops [3.2] or widows, are seen to lead lives which are above reproach.

*V*8: **But if any provideth not for his own, and specially his own household, he hath denied the faith, and is worse than an unbeliever.**

Paul's strong language appears to indicate that some in Ephesus were trying to evade the duty of supporting their own relatives by making the church responsible for them [*v* 4]. Such a man stands condemned on two counts: 1. he has denied 'the faith' in the practical sense of failing to fulfil the duties it inculcates [*Exod* 20.12]; 2. he is worse than an unbeliever not only because many pagans perform the duty [*Rom* 2.14], but also because he has the law of Christ to guide him [*Gal* 6.2, 10]. 'Faith does not set aside natural duties, but perfects and strengthens them' (Bengel). [*James* 2.14–17].

*V*9: **Let none be enrolled as a widow under threescore years old, *having been* the wife of one man, 10 well reported of for good works; if she hath brought up children, if she hath used hospitality to strangers, if she hath washed the saints' feet, if she hath relieved the afflicted, if she hath diligently followed every good work.**

To ensure that the generosity of the church is not abused, Paul next specifies the qualifications of 'true' widows [*v* 3]. No widow under the age of sixty is to be put on the list of those entitled to receive regular support. (Naturally this ruling would not prevent a younger widow from receiving whatever help was necessary in time of need.) As to her character, she must have been a faithful wife and be well known for her good works. 'The wife of one man' clearly cannot mean 'only once married', since the apostle advises younger widows to marry again [*v* 14; cf 3.2, 12]. What is meant by 'good works' is explained by the five examples which are introduced by the word 'if'. A widow who is worthy of the church's support will have brought up her children well (assuming she had a family), been given to hospitality and the attendant courtesy of washing her guests' feet, and in short, will have devoted herself to 'all kinds of good deeds' (NIV). Some have claimed that the passage already points to the enrolment of an 'official' order of widows, and that the list given in verse 10 even hints at their duties, despite the fact that the verbs used all refer to their past conduct! 'But there is no proper evidence whatever to show that such widows as those here mentioned by the apostle were invested with any sort of office, or were called to do anything but such pious and free-will service as their own hearts might prompt, and their limited opportunities might enable them to perform' (Fairbairn).

V 11: **But younger widows refuse: for when they have waxed wanton against Christ, they desire to marry; 12 having condemnation, because they have rejected their first pledge.**

With regard to younger widows, Paul directs Timothy to refuse to put them on the roll for permanent support, for when they are swayed by sensual desires that alienate them from Christ, they wish to marry. In view of the advice given in verse 14, the condemnation thus incurred could hardly be due to the rejection of a 'pledge' not to remarry. 'This is not an apostolic beginning of monastic orders. Paul is not in one breath keeping widows from remarriage and in the next breath urging this very thing' (Lenski). 'First pledge' literally means 'first faith' (ASV margin), and the particular danger envisaged is that a younger widow, in whom the sexual impulse is still strong, might allow her natural affection to override her first loyalty to Christ and marry a pagan. By entering into such a union, she would bring judgment upon herself, and disgrace upon the faithful community whose fellowship she had publicly renounced.

*V*13: **And withal they learn also** *to be* **idle, going about from house to house; and not only idle, but tattlers also and busybodies, speaking things which they ought not.**

Moreover, if younger widows were placed on the list for full support, this would encourage idleness and leave them free to gossip and meddle with affairs which were no concern of theirs. To warn Timothy of the undesirable consequences of such unwise charity, Paul draws a vivid picture of these young women gadding about from house to house, 'speaking of things better left unspoken' (NEB). 'As vagrants, or as pedlars opening their packs, and dropping here a tale and there a tale. A practice flatly forbidden by God, Levit 19.16, "Thou shalt not go up and down as a talebearer among thy people" ' (Trapp).

*V*14: **I desire therefore that the younger** *widows* **marry, bear children, rule the household, give no**

occasion to the adversary for reviling: 15 for already some are turned aside after Satan.

In view of these dangers, Paul counsels younger widows to marry, if, as the context makes clear [*vv* 11, 12], they can marry 'in the Lord' [1 *Cor* 7.39]. Then bringing up a family and managing the home will keep them so busy that 'the adversary' (i.e. the devil or his agents, cf 4.1) will be given no opportunity for slander. Paul's explanatory remark shows that he was not merely theorizing in verses 11–13, but speaking from sad experience. Some of the younger widows had already thrown off their allegiance to Christ and turned aside after Satan. 'Therefore the apostle would have them regarded as beacons, warning the church not to continue the over-indulgent treatment it had begun to exhibit toward such' (Fairbairn).

V 16: **If any woman that believeth hath widows, let her relieve them, and let not the church be burdened; that it may relieve them that are widows indeed.**

In rounding off his discussion of widows, Paul shows that the Christian woman with dependent widows in her family should support them and not let the church be burdened with them, so that the church can help those widows who are really destitute. This instruction would apply both to the woman whose husband was not a believer, and to the woman of means who managed her own household (like Lydia, *Acts* 16.14f). The longer reading of the AV – 'believer (masc.) or believer (fem.)' – was probably due to copyists who 'felt that a restriction of the principle of this verse to Christian women was unfair' (Bruce M. Metzger, *A Textual Commentary on the Greek New Testament*, p. 642).

*V*17: **Let the elders that rule well be counted worthy of double honour, especially those who labour in the word and in teaching.**

After showing how widows are to be honoured [*vv* 3–16], the apostle next enforces the duty of honouring the spiritual leaders of the church, who are here called 'elders' rather than 'overseers' to draw attention to the dignity of their position (cf comment on 3.1). The elders who rule well [3.4, 5] should be counted worthy of double honour, i.e. they should be honoured not only for the sake of their office, but also for the excellence of their work. This double honour applies especially to elders who are giving all their energies to preaching and teaching [3.2]. But if the primary meaning of 'honour' is to the fore, the next verse suggests that the idea of remuneration was also present in Paul's mind [*v* 18], for he 'was thinking particularly of the honour which the church was bound to show to their elders by presenting them with the means necessary for their support' (Huther).

*V*18: **For the scripture saith, Thou shalt not muzzle the ox when he treadeth out the corn. And, The labourer is worthy of his hire.**

As in 1 *Cor* 9.9, Paul's quotation of *Deut* 25.4 is an argument from the lesser to the greater: 'If God commands men to care for the oxen which tread out the corn, how much more does this principle hold good for ministers who labour to provide men with the Bread of Life?'

Although the second quotation is evidently introduced as a well-known saying of the Lord [*Luke* 10.7], we can not be sure that Paul intended to include it in the category of Scripture. But even if the opening formula applies only to the first quotation, the close connection ('and') shows that the words of Jesus had the same normative authority for the church as the written word of God, i.e. the Old Testament (cf comment on 4.13). On the other hand, Paul may have seen the original text of Luke's Gospel, in which case this 'would be the earliest instance of the Lord's words being quoted as "Scripture" ' (Lock).

*V*19: **Against an elder receive not an accusation, except at *the mouth of* two or three witnesses. 20 Them that sin reprove in the sight of all, that the rest also may be in fear.**

Since the ministry is a prime target for Satan's malice, no accusation against an elder is to be entertained without evidence from two or three witnesses [*Deut* 19.15; *Matt* 18.16; 2 *Cor* 13.1]. 'If to be accused were sufficient to make a man guilty, no good minister should be innocent . . . Truth hath always a scratcht face. Men hate him that reproveth in the gate. Every fool hath a bolt to shoot at a faithful preacher' (Trapp). But elders who are found guilty of sin must be publicly rebuked so that other believers ('the rest') may fear to follow their bad example. Paul is here speaking of sins that give rise to public scandal, for if any elder 'commits a fault not in that category, it is clearly preferable that he should be admonished privately rather than openly accused' (Calvin).

*V*21: **I charge *thee* in the sight of God, and Christ**

Jesus, and the elect angels, that thou observe these things without prejudice, doing nothing by partiality.

Paul solemnly charges Timothy to carry out the preceding disciplinary instructions with perfect fairness, neither prejudging the case nor showing any favouritism. As the apostle's every act is governed by his awareness of the divine presence, he fittingly reminds Timothy that his administration of the church comes under heavenly scrutiny. For every church leader needs to be reminded that his conduct is witnessed by 'God *and* Christ Jesus, *and* the elect angels'. The first 'and' joins God with Christ as divine, while the second marks off 'the elect angels' as creatures who owe their existence to God. The angels of heaven are here described as 'elect' in contrast to the fallen angels, 'who did not keep their position of authority but abandoned their own home' [*Jude* 6, NIV].

*V*22: **Lay hands hastily on no man, neither be partaker of other men's sins: keep thyself pure.**

Do not be over-hasty in laying on hands in ordination, or you may find yourself responsible for other people's misdeeds; keep your own hands clean. (NEB) Paul here impresses upon Timothy the importance of ensuring that only men of unquestioned integrity are appointed to the ministry. For if he neglects to guard this holy office against profane intruders, he may find himself sharing the blame for their sins. It is as he thus seeks to preserve the purity of the church that he will keep himself pure. This seems to be the primary meaning of the final clause, though a more general reference cannot be ruled

[79]

out. Some interpreters maintain that this laying on of hands refers to the formal restoration of penitents to membership, 'but there is no trace in the New Testament of the existence of this custom in apostolic times' (Huther). [cf 4.14; 2 *Tim* 1.6].

*V*23: **Be no longer a drinker of water, but use a little wine for thy stomach's sake and thine often infirmities.**

Perhaps a desire to clarify the preceding exhortation ('keep thyself pure') prompted the apostle to warn Timothy against practising self-discipline at the expense of his health. Apparently Timothy drank only water in case others should think he was addicted to wine [3.2]. But in view of Timothy's frequent ailments, Paul urges him to take a little wine as a remedy for these infirmities. 'How few there are today who need to be forbidden water, how many rather that need to be restricted to drinking wine soberly!' (Calvin).

*V*24: **Some men's sins are evident, going before unto judgment; and some men also they follow after. 25 In like manner also there are good works that are evident; and such as are otherwise cannot be hid.**

These general statements resume the thought of verse 22. Although the wise choosing of elders is undoubtedly difficult, the task will be made much easier if Timothy remembers that conduct always affords the best guide to character. Paul first describes those who are unfit for office. The sins of some men are so obvious that they rush before them to judgment, proclaiming their guilt in advance; whereas 'there are others whose offences have not yet overtaken them' (NEB), but careful enquiry will usually succeed in bringing them to light. Similarly, fitness for office is made evident by good works, which cannot remain hidden, even if they are not immediately apparent. If Timothy bears these guidelines in mind, he will ensure that unworthy men are not ordained and that good men are not overlooked.

CHAPTER SIX

*The apostle directs Christian slaves to honour their masters so
that the gospel is not dishonoured, while those with believing
masters must not presume upon the bond of Christian love but
should serve them even better [vv 1, 2]. The proud corrupters
of the true faith are next denounced, for they not only engage in
sterile controversies, but also make their religion a pretext for
gain. The real gain of godliness with contentment is contrasted
with the illusory pursuit of riches, which has proved to be the
root of all kinds of evil for many [vv 3–10]. Paul charges
Timothy to fight the good fight of faith, and to witness a good
confession without reproach as he keeps in view the approaching
advent of Christ, whose appearing shall reveal the full glory of
the world's only Ruler [vv 11–16]. Wealthy believers must not
trust in uncertain riches, but are exhorted to be rich in those good
works by which they can lay up for themselves true treasure in
heaven [vv 17–19]. Paul's final appeal urges Timothy to guard
the deposit, and to shun the profane sophistries which have
ensnared some, while his closing benediction embraces the whole
church [vv 20–21].*

V 1: **Let as many as are servants under the yoke count
their own masters worthy of all honour, that the
name of God and the doctrine be not blasphemed. 2
And they that have believing masters, let them not**

despise them, because they are brethren; but let them serve them the rather, because they that partake of the benefit are believing and beloved. These things teach and exhort.

In dealing with the delicate question of the attitude to be adopted by converted slaves towards their masters, Paul neither preaches revolutionary change nor even a resigned acceptance of the *status quo*, but reminds them of the importance of their position as ambassadors of the gospel [cf *Titus* 2.10]. Hence all who are under the yoke as slaves should not only bow to the authority of their unbelieving masters, but also regard them as worthy of all respect. For while such ungrudging service will commend the gospel they profess, 'the name of God' would be blasphemed if pagans 'could point to Christians doing their ordinary duties badly as the effect of their religion' (Parry). In those cases where Christian slaves are blessed in having believing masters, they must not behave as though their equality before God had erased the civil distinction between them. Instead of despising or looking down on their masters, they should serve them all the better, 'because those who benefit from their service are believers, and dear to them' (NIV). Timothy must continue to teach and exhort 'these things' concerning the duty of slaves, so that the church might not be charged with undermining the foundations of society by encouraging a rebellious spirit in slaves.

*V*3: **If any man teacheth a different doctrine, and consenteth not to sound words, *even* the words of our Lord Jesus Christ, and to the doctrine which is according to godliness; 4 he is puffed up, knowing nothing, but doting about questionings and disputes**

of words, whereof cometh envy, strife, railings, evil surmisings, 5 wranglings of men corrupted in mind and bereft of the truth, supposing that godliness is a way of gain.

The warmth of Paul's words here shows how far removed he is from the Laodicean indifference of the modern church towards those who teach a 'different' doctrine which is quite alien to the apostolic faith [cf *Gal* 1.6–9]. According to the apostle, the church must reject any one whose teaching does not agree with the healthy words '*of* our Lord Jesus Christ', for that is the only doctrine which is in conformity with and conducive to godliness [*Titus* 1.1]. The reference is not to the words spoken directly by the Lord, but to the fact that the exalted Christ is both the ultimate *source* of the apostles' doctrine and the great *subject* of all their preaching.

he is puffed up with conceit, he knows nothing; he has a morbid craving for controversy and for disputes about words, (RSV) Paul next provides Timothy with a penetrating analysis of the 'psychology of error' (Lenski). The false teacher is inflated with the pride that blinds him to the truth, but though he knows nothing as it really is, he does not hesitate to confine the entire cosmos within the strait-jacket of his preconceived ideas. Instead of delighting in the healthy words of the gospel, he is morbidly absorbed with useless speculations and hair-splitting 'disputes about words' (our 'logomachies'). 'The wit of heretics and schismatics will better serve them to devise a thousand shifts to elude the truth than their pride will suffer them once to yield and acknowledge it' (Trapp).

that result in envy, quarrelling, malicious talk, evil suspicions and constant friction between men of corrupt mind, who have been robbed of the truth and who think that godliness is a means to financial gain.
(NIV) Paul lists five social consequences which stem from the mind that is diseased by pride: 1. 'envy', provoked by more brilliant speculations; 2. 'quarrelling' with the proponents of these theories; 3. 'malicious talk', the slandering of such rivals; 4. 'evil suspicions', doubting the honesty of those who beg to differ from them; 5. 'constant friction', the mutual irritation which exists between those who propagate contrary errors. Although these false teachers were once acquainted with the truth, they were never possessed by it, and have now been defrauded of any interest in it through the innate depravity of their minds. The essential secularity of their thought is demonstrated by their mercenary motives. They care neither for God nor man, but simply don the mask of religion in order to enrich themselves [*Titus* 1.11].

*V*6: **But godliness with contentment is great gain: 7 for we brought nothing into the world, for neither can we carry anything out; 8 but having food and covering we shall be therewith content.**

But if godliness is not a gainful trade, there *is* great gain in the godliness which is coupled with 'contentment' [cf 4.8]. The word literally means 'self-sufficiency', and it was used by the Cynics and Stoics to describe the wise man whose inner resources make him independent of all outside help. What the word means to Paul is made plain in *Phil* 4.11–13. 'Godliness is ever accompanied with contentment in a greater or lesser degree; all truly godly people have

learned with St Paul, in whatever state they are, to be
therewith content' (Matthew Henry). It is evident that
such a lack of dependence upon worldly possessions is the
only reasonable attitude for believers to adopt (note the
three 'we' verbs). For we brought nothing into the world,
and we can take nothing out of it [*Job* 1:21; *Eccles* 5.15].
'Whatever a man amasses by the way is in the nature of
luggage, no part of his truest personality, but something
he leaves behind at the toll-bar of death' (E. K. Simpson).
So if we have food and shelter, we shall be content with
these necessaries and not hanker after luxuries. 'For nature
is content with a little and all that goes beyond natural
usage is superfluous. Not that a more liberal use of
possessions should be condemned as bad in itself, but a
desire for it is always sinful' (Calvin)

*V*9: **But they that are minded to be rich fall into a
temptation and a snare and many foolish and hurtful
lusts, such as drown men in destruction and perdition.**

Those who have fixed their desires upon wealth as their
highest good soon find they are following a downward
path, which brings them sorrow in this world and eternal
perdition in the next. In falling a prey to this temptation,
they are caught like an animal in a trap, and are held fast
by 'many foolish and hurtful lusts'. 'The desires in question
are foolish, because they cannot be logically defended;
they are hurtful, because they hinder true happiness'
(White). Such lusts plunge men into 'destruction and
perdition'. 'The combination (found only here) is
emphatic, "loss for time and eternity"' (Lock).

[86]

V 10: **For the love of money is a root of all kinds of evil: which some reaching after have been led astray from the faith, and have pierced themselves through with many sorrows.**

Although money is not in itself evil, the *love* of money is a root of all kinds of evil. 'The sentiment is, that there is no kind of evil to which the love of money may not lead men, when it once fairly takes hold of them' (Fairbairn). In thus reaching after money 'some have wandered away from the faith and pierced their hearts with many pangs' (RSV). A departure from the faith is inevitable when gold displaces God in man's affections, and Paul clearly knows some in Ephesus who have exchanged spiritual treasure for material wealth with tragic consequences to themselves [*Matt* 6.24]. For instead of gaining joy and satisfaction from their riches, they suffer the pangs of conscience and the anguish of disillusionment. 'Many a millionaire, after choking his soul with gold-dust, has died from melancholia!' (Simpson).

V 11: **But thou, O man of God, flee these things; and follow after righteousness, godliness, faith, love, patience, meekness.**

Paul bases this personal appeal to Timothy upon an emphatic reminder of what he is by the grace of God: 'But *thou*, O man of God'. The title was given to Old Testament prophets and is especially appropriate to one who is called to serve God in the ministry of the gospel, though obviously this does not mean that other Christians are to be something less than this [cf 2 *Tim* 3.17]. As befits a man of God, Timothy is ever to flee 'these things', i.e. the

[87]

love of money and its attendant evils. On the positive side, he must be constant in his pursuit of the Christian virtues. The six named here fall into three pairs. 1. 'Righteousness' and 'godliness' cover the whole of the Christian's duty: upright conduct towards man, and reverent devotion towards God. 2. 'Faith' and 'love' are linked together as the animating principles of the Christian life. 3. 'Patient endurance' and 'meekness' denote the conduct proper to a Christian amid the enmity and opposition of the world to Christ's gospel, 'the former being opposed to submission, the latter to exasperation' (Huther) [cf 2 *Tim* 2.25].

*V*12: **Fight the good fight of the faith, lay hold on the life eternal, whereunto thou wast called, and didst confess the good confession in the sight of many witnesses.**

Fight the good fight of faith, (AV) Having hinted at the need for perseverance and strenuous effort, Paul now exhorts Timothy to fight the good fight 'which faith in a man wages against all that hinders and opposes; not a fight for "the faith" as against false teachers, but faith's fight for the prize of the high calling' (Parry) [1 *Cor* 9.24f.; *Phil* 3.12f.].

lay hold on the life eternal, This cannot be the reward bestowed at the end of the contest, since Timothy is urged to grasp eternal life even while he continues to fight the good fight. But in realizing by faith what he possesses in Christ, he can live a life which is *qualitatively* different from his former walk, and this is because the future has already invaded his present experience [cf 4.8].

[88]

to which you were called when you made the good confession in the presence of many witnesses. (RSV) As the context shows that the calling in view is that to salvation and not service, these words must refer to Timothy's baptism rather than his ordination (see the further comment on the next verse).

*V*13: **I charge thee in the sight of God, who giveth life to all things, and of Christ Jesus, who before Pontius Pilate witnessed the good confession; 14 that thou keep the commandment, without spot, without reproach, until the appearing of our Lord Jesus Christ:**

The credal content of this solemn charge to Timothy has led scholars to suggest that Paul is here citing part of a baptismal confession (note the reference to God as Creator, and to Christ's witness before Pilate and his second coming in judgment). In the primitive church baptism was preceded by careful instruction in the faith, and was administered in the presence of the congregation when the candidates were required to make a public profession of their faith in Christ [*v* 12; *Rom* 10.9; 1 *Cor* 12.3; *Phil* 2.11]. Now just as Timothy had confessed at his baptism, 'Jesus is Lord', so Jesus had made the same 'good confession' by witnessing to his own kingship before Pilate [*Mark* 15.2]. The commandment which must be kept 'without spot, without reproach' is therefore 'the charge laid on Timothy in his baptism, for the once-for-all confession of obedience to the divine Lord made in baptism can fittingly be appealed to at any subsequent time' (G. R. Beasley-Murray, *Baptism in the New Testament*, pp. 205–6). Although the 'appearing' of Christ in glory was always at the forefront of Paul's thought, he never pretended to know the date of the Lord's return, but is content to affirm that it will occur at the appropriate time determined by God (*v* 15, 'which God will bring about in his own time', NIV).

*V*15: **which in its own times he shall show, who is the blessed and only Potentate, the King of kings, and Lord of lords; 16 who only hath immortality, dwelling in light unapproachable; whom no man hath seen, nor can see: to whom *be* honour and power eternal. Amen.**

If the time of Christ's appearing is fixed by God, then every intervening event must also be under his sovereign control, and this leads Paul into a magnificent outburst of praise which expands the thought of his opening doxology [cf 1.17].

who is the blessed and only Potentate, The first epithet describes the absolute bliss which God possesses in himself; the second, the absolute sovereignty of his power over all things.

the King of kings, and Lord of lords, i.e. 'the King of those reigning and the Lord of those ruling'. 'He means that the powers of this world are subject to His supreme dominion, depend upon Him, and stand or fall at His will' (Calvin).

who only hath immortality, 'He only has immortality; he only is immortal in himself, and has immortality as he is the Fountain of it, for the immortality of angels and spirits is derived from him' (Matthew Henry).

dwelling in light unapproachable; God dwells in a realm of light of such dazzling radiance that mortal man can neither approach nor apprehend him [cf *Ps* 104.2].

whom no man hath seen, nor can see: 'Even a beatific vision of heaven will not consist of a sight of God as God, but rather as He shines forth in a manifestative and communicative way in the person of Christ, as suited to finite capacities' (Arthur Pink). [*Exod* 33.20; *John* 1.18].

to whom be honour and power eternal. Amen. Paul concludes this sublime doxology by ascribing honour and power to God, as the One who is supremely worthy of all worship and praise, and he seals it with the solemn word of confirmation ('Amen' = 'so be it').

*V*17: **Charge them that are rich in this present world, that they be not highminded, nor have their hope set on the uncertainty of riches, but on God, who giveth us richly all things to enjoy;** 18 **that they do good, that they be rich in good works, that they be ready to distribute, willing to communicate;** 19 **laying up in store for themselves a good foundation against the time to come, that they may lay hold on the life which is** *life* **indeed.**

Paul now returns to the subject of riches [*vv* 9, 10], and outlines the instruction Timothy must give to believers who are rich, as wealth is reckoned 'in this present world'. 1. Regarding the dangers to be avoided: he is to charge

them not to be high-minded, to prevent them from
becoming 'purse-proud' and looking down on their poorer
brethren; he is to warn them not to have their hope set on
'uncertain' riches [*Prov* 23.5], but on God 'who endows
us richly with all things to enjoy' (NEB). Clearly this is a
shaft directed against the ascetic demands of the heretics
[4.1–5]. 'No good purpose is served by pretending that
God did not intend us to enjoy the pleasurable sensations
of physical life' (White). 2. Regarding the duties to be
enjoined: he is to charge them to do good and be rich in
good works, which means they must be ready to share
their wealth and be quick to recognize the claims of
Christian fellowship. In this way they will lay up treasure
for themselves as a firm foundation for the future, so that
they may grasp that which is life indeed [cf *Matt* 6.19,
20]. Paul's teaching here 'is in exact accord with Christ's
in *Matt* 25.34–40, 46b. Salvation, to be sure, is entirely *by
grace through faith* [*Eph* 2.8; *Titus* 3.5], but the reward is
according to works [*Dan* 12.3; 2 *Cor* 5.10; *Rev* 20.12]'
(William Hendriksen).

*V*20: **O Timothy, guard that which is committed
unto *thee*, turning away from the profane babblings
and oppositions of the knowledge which is falsely so
called; 21 which some professing have erred concerning the faith.**

Grace be with you.

Paul virtually sums up the message of the Epistle in his
final appeal to Timothy, which was probably written in
his own hand [2 *Thess* 3.17].

O Timothy, guard the deposit which is committed unto *thee*, (ASV margin). Paul earnestly exhorts Timothy to guard that 'deposit' (i.e. the 'sound doctrine' of the gospel), which has been entrusted to his safe-keeping. 'What is a deposit? It is something that is accredited to thee, not invented by thee; something that thou hast received, not that thou hast thought out; a result not of genius but of instruction; not of personal ownership but of public tradition; a matter brought to thee, not produced by thee, with respect to which thou art bound to be not an author but a custodian, not an originator but a bearer, not a leader but a follower' (Vincent of Lérins: 5th century).

turning away from the profane babblings and oppositions of the knowledge which is falsely so called; On the negative side Timothy is to spurn the empty chatter which opposes the true gospel in the name of 'knowledge' [cf 1.3, 4]. 'Any speculation, any philosophizing, any form of learning, any scientific theorizing which sought to intrude itself, in the way of modifying it in the least respect, upon the Gospel of Christ, – which is a sacred deposit committed to its ministers not to dilute or to alter or to modify, but to learn, hold, guard and preach, – would be characterized by Paul without hesitation as among the profane inanities and contradictions of knowledge falsely so called' (B. B. Warfield, 'The Inviolate Deposit', *Faith and Life*, p. 388).

which some professing have missed the mark concerning the faith. (ASV margin) This is another veiled reference to the false teachers [cf 1.19]. 'In their profession of a knowledge which was secular in its method and shallow in its character, they failed in maintaining their own faith in GOD revealed in Christ, the only sure qualification for true knowledge' (Parry).

Grace be with you. Paul uses the plural 'you' in this brief benediction, because he knew that his letter to Timothy would also be read to the church at Ephesus.

TITUS

CHAPTER ONE

In greeting Titus as his true son in the faith, Paul also describes the content of the message entrusted to him [vv 1–4]. Titus was left in Crete to set things in order and appoint elders, who must be good men and able teachers of sound doctrine [vv 5–9]. The character given to the Cretans by one of their own poets is exemplified by the deceivers who spread the leaven of legalism for base gain. Titus must rebuke them sharply that they may be sound in the faith, for though their Jewish mentors professed to know God, their evil deeds proved that they were strangers to the truth [vv 10–16].

V1: **Paul, a servant of God, and an apostle of Jesus Christ, according to the faith of God's elect, and the knowledge of the truth which is according to godliness,**

Instead of a brief personal greeting to a trusted associate, we have here a lengthy salutation whose official tone suggests that it was intended by Paul to provide Titus with the necessary authorization for his mission in Crete [vv 1–4]. In calling himself 'a servant of God', Paul indicates his complete submission to the divine will, and in claiming the title 'an apostle of Jesus Christ', he points to the commission he received from Christ, who sent him forth as his messenger to the Gentiles [*Acts* 22.21]. Paul's service and apostleship are in perfect accord with the elect's faith and knowledge of the truth. So if the Cretans are indeed God's elect, their faith and knowledge will be in harmony with the testimony of Christ's own apostle, for that is the only doctrine 'which is according to godliness'. By thus insisting upon the essential connection between faith and godliness, Paul at once strikes the keynote of the Epistle and tacitly condemns the ungodly myths peddled by the false teachers. As God chose us to be holy [*Eph* 1.4], the only convincing evidence of our election is found in that life of godliness which is the fruit of faith [2 *Pet* 1.5–10].

*V*2: **in hope of eternal life, which God, who cannot lie, promised before times eternal; 3 but in his own seasons manifested his word in the message, wherewith I was intrusted according to the commandment of God our Saviour;**

As an apostle of Jesus Christ, Paul takes his stand on 'the hope of eternal life', which inspires all his labours and enables him to endure present afflictions cheerfully [cf 2 *Tim* 1.1; 1 *Cor* 15.19]. In contrast to the untruthful Cretans [*v* 12], God who cannot lie [I *Sam* 15.29], promised this eternal life from all eternity [cf 2 *Tim* 1.9]. The reference is to the pre-temporal purpose of God. As the covenant of redemption was ratified before the creation of the world [John 17.24], so the time of its manifestation is appointed by the divine decree [*Gal* 4.4; *Eph* 1.10]. This revelation of God's word is made in the message of the gospel, which Paul emphatically claims was entrusted to him, 'according to the commandment

of God our Saviour' [*Eph* 3.8; 1 *Tim* 1.11–13]. The
Cretan errorists can claim no such authority for their
perverse deviations from the truth. The designation of
God as '*our* Saviour' is strongly confessional, and it
challenges the church in Crete to remain true to the
apostolic faith. The clear teaching of this passage is that
no man should take upon himself any office in the church
without *God's* call. 'Whoever would find comfort in
themselves, or clear and justify their callings to others,
or do good in the place of the body where they are set,
they must be able to prove that they are not intruders
but called by this calling and commandment of God. As
Paul performed every duty in the church by virtue of his
extraordinary calling, so they must by virtue of their
ordinary' (Thomas Taylor).

*V*4: **to Titus, my true child after a common faith:
Grace and peace from God the Father and Christ
Jesus our Saviour.**

The intimate address 'my true child after a common
faith' implies that Titus had been converted through
Paul's ministry. The faith they shared was the faith
common to all the elect, as opposed to the disruptive
Jewish myths spread abroad by the heretics. A Gentile by
birth, Titus probably became a Christian during the
mission to Antioch [*Acts* 11.25, 26; *Gal* 2.1–3]. The
otherwise unaccountable omission of his name from Acts
lends plausibility to the suggestion that he was a relative
of Luke (cf W. M. Ramsay *St. Paul the Traveller and the
Roman citizen*, p. 390). Be that as it may, it is clear from
his success at troubled Corinth that Titus was endowed
with the right qualities to deal with the difficult situation

in Crete [2 *Cor* 2.13; 7.6–15; 8.6, 16–18; 12.18]. As usual in Paul, the greeting 'Grace and peace' denotes the undeserved favour of God and the spiritual well-being that flows from it. These divine blessings are conjointly bestowed by God the Father and Christ Jesus 'our Saviour'. The title applied to the Father in the previous verse is here transferred to Christ, since our salvation is equally the gift of the Father's electing love and Christ's redeeming work.

*V*5: **For this cause left I thee in Crete, that thou shouldest set in order the things that were wanting, and appoint elders in every city, as I gave thee charge;**

'As I gave thee charge' shows that Paul is not giving Titus a new directive, but providing him with the written authorization for the task already laid upon him. First, he is to 'straighten out what was left unfinished' (NIV). This would include checking the false teachers, and instructing believers in the doctrine that promotes godliness [1.10, 11; 2.1–10]. Secondly, he is to appoint elders in every city. The method of selection is not specified, but probably Titus would encourage each congregation to choose suitable men whose appointment he would then formally confirm [cf *Acts* 14.23]. As in 1 *Tim* 3.2ff., Paul emphasizes the moral qualities which are required in those who are to lead the flock. 'The danger was lest talent and cleverness should carry the day, and the leadership of the Church fall into the hands of men deficient in the elements of a worthy Christian character . . . Self-seeking teachers had insinuated themselves into the Christian societies, who knew how to impose on the credulous or unstable by their show of learning and asceticism . . . Entrance into the ministry must be barred to such candidates as these; and officers must be chosen whose character commanded the respect of the community, and who would be likely to exert a wholesome and steadying influence on the Church's life, at a time of transition and feverish unrest' (Findlay).

*V*6: **if any man is blameless, the husband of one wife, having children that believe, who are not accused of riot or unruly.**

The qualifications for elders are very similar to those given in 1 *Tim* 3.1–7, but the fact that deacons are not mentioned here suggests that the organization of the church in Crete was less advanced than at Ephesus. Although God has committed the treasure of the gospel to earthen vessels, they must be *clean* vessels if their testimony is to be effective. The message proclaimed with the lips lacks all credibility unless it is first embodied in the life. Thus the character must be in accord with the calling: a man who is blameless, a faithful husband (see comment on 1 *Tim* 3.2), and a wise father (see comment on 1 *Tim* 3.4, 5). Since older men were chosen as elders, their suitability could best be gauged by the way in which they had brought up their children [*Prov* 22.6]. Paul only wants men with believing children, and not men whose children have a reputation for profligacy or disobedience.

*V*7: **For the bishop must be blameless, as God's steward; not self-willed, not soon angry, no brawler, no striker, not greedy of filthy lucre;**

The sudden switch from 'elder' to 'bishop' proves that they are interchangeable terms, the first denoting the office, and the second describing the function (see comment on 1 *Tim* 3.1). The 'bishop' or overseer must be blameless because he is the steward of *God's* household, the church [cf 1 *Tim* 3.15]. Paul defines what it means to be 'blameless' in a series of five negatives [*v* 7] and seven positives [*vv* 8, 9]. On the negative side, a representative list is given of the vices which the worker in God's household must not have: 1. he will not arrogantly insist on having his own way without any regard to the opinions of others; 2. he will not be quick-tempered since pastoral work requires great patience; 3. he will not be given to much wine (see comment on 1 *Tim* 3.3); 4. he will not strike his opponents with blows or with words; 5. he will not be motivated by a desire for base gain, either by making his teaching the means of enriching himself (as the heretics did, *v* 11), or by misappropriating church funds (as Judas did, *John* 12.6).

*V*8: **but given to hospitality, a lover of good, sober-minded, just, holy, self-controlled;**

On the positive side the bishop will be: 1. hospitable (see comment on 1 *Tim* 3.2); 2. a lover of what is good, whether good men, good deeds, or good things; 3. well-disciplined in thought and behaviour; 4. just in all his dealings with others; 5. devout in his dedication to God; 6. self-controlled because Spirit-filled [cf *Gal* 5.23].

*V*9: **holding to the faithful word which is according to the teaching, that he may be able both to exhort in the sound doctrine, and to convict the gainsayers.**

Lastly, the Christian minister must hold fast to the trustworthy word which is in accordance with the apostolic teaching [cf *Rom* 6.17: 'the pattern of teaching'], 'so that he can encourage others by sound doctrine and refute those who oppose it' (NIV). Only 'the truth, the whole truth, and nothing but the truth' is equal to the twofold task of building up the faithful and exposing the errors of its adversaries. Calvin warns against the dangerous fickleness 'whereby a pastor does not steadfastly maintain the doctrine of which he should be the unshaken protagonist. In short, there is required in a pastor not only learning but such zeal for pure doctrine that he will never depart from it'.

V 10: **For there are many unruly men, vain talkers and deceivers, specially they of the circumcision,** 11 **whose mouths must be stopped; men who overthrow whole houses, teaching things which they ought not, for filthy lucre's sake.**

It appears that there were many self-appointed teachers within the church, especially Jewish Christians, whose erroneous doctrines were undermining the faith of whole families [cf *2 Tim* 3.6]. Paul wisely refrains from repeating their false teaching, but roundly denounces them as rebels who flout the authority of the church by the voluble but empty rhetoric which deceives the unwary. 'Note the difference between these and godly pastors, who are according to God's heart. They feed God's people with wisdom and understanding, while the other feed with vanity and wind; these have their gifts and calling from God, and speak every word from Him and for Him; the other, like the Devil's cooks, are ever blending impurities with the truth, that it may be never purely tasted. Like untrusty solicitors, they speak one word for God and two for themselves' (Taylor). The mouths of these men must be muzzled, so that no further damage is done to the church [cf 1 *Tim* 1.3, 4]. Finally, the duplicity of such falsehood is revealed by its motivation. For whereas the true shepherds preach the truth for its own sake, the emissaries of error do their deadly work 'for filthy lucre's sake'. 'If Balaam's eye is upon Balak's gold, it must needs be blinded; and when covetousness has become the conscience of men, no wonder if they speak, write, or attempt anything, if it will help them forward to their expected wages' (Taylor).

*V*12: **One of themselves, a prophet of their own, said, Cretans are always liars, evil beasts, idle gluttons.**

In quoting the testimony of Epimenides, whom the Cretans revered as a prophet, Paul has his readers on the horns of a dilemma. They must either agree with this verdict on their character, or repudiate the charge and make their own seer a liar. In fact the Cretan reputation for lying was so notorious in the ancient world that the verb 'to Cretize' meant 'to lie and cheat'. As to the ferocity of the Cretans, Epimenides also said that the absence of wild beasts from Crete was supplied by its human inhabitants! The further stigma 'idle gluttons' accuses them of the laziness that desires satisfaction without the exertion of earning an honest living. The character given to the Cretans by this heathen poet is exemplified by the errorists who spread Jewish myths for base gain [*vv* 13, 14].

[104]

*V*13: **This testimony is true. For which cause reprove them sharply, that they may be sound in the faith,**

Paul endorses the truth of this saying, and therefore instructs Titus to administer a sharp reproof to 'the gainsayers' [*v* 9]. Because their false teaching threatened the whole church, the severity of the rebuke must be equal to the gravity of the danger, both to those they deceived and to themselves as the self-deceived [cf 2 *Tim* 3.13]. But though the disease calls for drastic treatment, the true surgeon of souls only cuts to achieve a cure. There is a remedial purpose in view. It is 'that they may be sound in the faith'. 'Much vituperation would have been saved had Christians always had this saving purpose in mind when dealing with those erring from the faith' (Guthrie).

*V*14: **not giving heed to Jewish fables, and commandments of men who turn away from the truth.**

Paul next diagnoses the source of this disease. It arises from professed Christians giving heed to a form of teaching which is quite alien to the gospel. To insist on preserving the purity of the faith may seem unadventurous to some, but it is impossible to improve what is fixed and final by the addition of a medley of Jewish myths and human regulations [cf 3.9 and see comment on 1 *Tim* 1.3, 6]. 'God's truth must not thus be bartered for the fallacies and fables of men. Fallible sanctions cannot usurp the place of infallible' (Simpson). The Cretan deceivers had learned their aberrations from men who persisted in rejecting the truth, i.e. from Jews whose

[105]

ascetic demands were probably not unlike those reflected in the Colossian 'heresy' [*Col* 2.22 and see Introduction].

*V*15: **To the pure all things are pure: but to them that are defiled and unbelieving nothing is pure; but both their mind and their conscience are defiled.**

The apostle here affirms the principle, 'To the pure all things are pure', in order to repudiate the prohibitions insisted upon by these outside teachers, whose defiled conscience led them to regard as unclean things which were in themselves capable of pure use [1 *Tim* 4.4; cf *Luke* 11.41; *Rom* 14.20; 1 *Cor* 6.12, 10.23]. Purity is not promoted by the ritualistic scruples of the Jewish legalists, who contaminate everything they touch because both their mind and conscience are polluted by unbelief. 'Since in God's sight there is no purity apart from faith, it follows that unbelievers are all unclean. Thus they will not obtain the cleanness they desire by any laws or regulations, for being themselves impure, nothing in the world can be pure to them' (Calvin).

*V*16: **They profess that they know God; but by their works they deny him, being abominable, and disobedient, and unto every good work reprobate.**

Paul has already branded the Jewish controversialists as 'men who turn away from the truth' [*v* 14], but because they professed to know God, they were able to palm off their errors on the self-appointed teachers within the church [*v* 13]. Whereas Paul hopes that a sharp reproof may restore the latter to soundness in the faith, he unsparingly condemns the unconverted outsiders whose fair words are belied by their evil deeds. Such men are 'abominable' or detestable in the sight of God, because they are 'disobedient' in their resolve to cling to the traditions of men rather than yield to the truth of the gospel, and are therefore disqualified from doing anything good. 'This last is like a final judgment. Like coins or metals that are tested as to genuineness these confessors of God are found spurious, utterly to be rejected' (Lenski).

CHAPTER TWO

In contrast to such errors, Titus must insist upon conduct that is
consistent with the sound teaching. Paul outlines the behaviour
expected of each group within the community, and urges Titus
to exercise a model ministry [vv 1–10]. For the grace of God
which brings salvation teaches men to renounce sin and to lead
godly lives as they look for the return of Christ, who died to
make his people zealous of good works. Titus is to teach these
things with all authority so that none may despise him [vv
11–15].

V1: But speak thou the things which befit the sound doctrine:

In contrast to the disease of heresy, Titus must continue
to speak what befits sound doctrine, for wholesome teaching promotes the spiritual health which is manifested in
an obedient walk [cf 1 Tim 1.10]. 'Christianity is primarily, indeed, a doctrine, but only that it may be in the true
sense a life; and the two can never be kept apart from each
other in the public teaching of the church without immi-
nent peril to both' (Fairbairn).

V2: that aged men be temperate, grave, sober-minded, sound in faith, in love, in patience:

The older men of the church are to set an example of spiritual maturity which is in keeping with their age. Titus should exhort them to be: 1. 'temperate', not given to excess of any kind; 2. 'grave', possessing the dignity that is worthy of respect; 3. 'sober-minded' or self-controlled [cf 1.8]; 4. 'sound in faith, in love, in patient endurance', personal qualities which would have a stabilizing influence in a community disturbed by false teaching.

V 3: **that aged women likewise be reverent in demeanour, not slanderers nor enslaved to much wine, teachers of that which is good;**

Similarly, the older women are to conduct themselves in a manner which is proper to their holy calling, so that 'their very walk and motion, their countenance, speech, silence, may present a certain dignity of holy propriety' (Jerome). The two negatives, 'not slanderers nor enslaved to much wine', point to the attendant dangers of indulging the Cretan penchant for idleness [1.12]. They should rather fill their time by being 'teachers of that which is good'. This does not refer to public instruction, but to the informal advice and help they can give to the younger women, by word and example [*vv* 4, 5].

V 4: **that they may train the young women to love their husbands, to love their children, 5 *to be* sober-minded, chaste, workers at home, kind, being in subjection to their own husbands, that the word of God be not blasphemed:**

Paul shows a fine regard for what is proper in delegating to older women the duty of training young women in their domestic duties. In view of the crucial effect of her influence upon society, Paul lists seven characteristics which are essential to the key rôle of the Christian wife and mother. The first pair are also first in importance: she is to be devoted to her husband and children, for such love will inspire and make light of every other duty. The second pair – 'sober-minded, chaste' – designate the self-control and purity which is to inform all her conduct. The third pair specify that she is to fulfil her household duties with kindness, for where this is lacking even the most efficient house-keeping is a doubtful boon. Finally, Paul requires wives to be subject to their own husbands, because it had to be shown that the natural relation between husband and wife was perfected rather than annulled by grace [*Eph* 5.22, 23; *Col* 3.18]. The final clause probably qualifies all seven items: 'that the word of God be not blasphemed' [cf *Is* 52.5; 1 *Tim* 6.1]. 'If the observed effect of the Gospel were to make women worse wives it would not commend it to the heathen' (White).

*V*6: **the younger men likewise exhort to be sober-minded:**

As a young man himself, Titus is instructed to urge the younger men to be self-controlled, and to show them what this means by his own example [*vv* 7, 8]. The admonition is brief, but comprehensive in its scope. For the greatest need of young men is to have their natural impetuosity firmly curbed by a prudent self-restraint.

*V*7: **in all things showing thyself an ensample of good works; in thy doctrine** *showing* **uncorruptness, gravity, 8 sound speech, that cannot be condemned; that**

he that is of the contrary part may be ashamed, having no evil thing to say of us.

As a minister of the gospel, Titus must be concerned about his public image. In all things he must strive to show himself as an example of good works, for his witness will not be effective unless his teaching is visibly embodied in his life. His teaching is to be marked by two important personal qualities. 'Uncorruptness' or 'soundness' expresses 'the single-mindedness and sincerity which a teacher of sacred things should exhibit. It signifies his whole-heartedness, while *gravity* rather has reference to his outward demeanour' (Bernard). The content of his teaching must be in conformity with the apostolic 'deposit' [2 *Tim* 1.14]: 'sound' or healthy speech which cannot be condemned, so that any opponent will be shamed into silence. By adding 'having no evil thing to say of *us*', Paul reminds Titus that any failure on his part would also reflect on the apostle whom he represented in Crete.

*V*9: *Exhort* **servants to be in subjection to their own masters, *and* to be well-pleasing *to them* in all things; not gainsaying;** 10 **not purloining, but showing all good fidelity; that they may adorn the doctrine of God our Saviour in all things.**

Christian slaves must be taught to give their masters satisfactory service by obeying them in all things. This will involve the avoidance of two vices to which slaves were especially prone: 1. 'not gainsaying', not answering back; 2. 'not purloining', not taking their masters' property for themselves. With reference to the latter, Humphreys remarks, 'Almost all trades, arts, and professions were at this time in the hands of slaves; and so all tricks of trade, all mercantile or professional embezzlement and dishonesty, are covered by the word'. But believers must show themselves to be so trustworthy that they may in all respects adorn the doctrine of God our Saviour. As the word 'adorn' is used of the setting of a jewel, to 'adorn the doctrine' means that it will be 'set off', and exhibited in a favourable light by the faithful conduct of those who profess it (so Bernard).

V 11: **For the grace of God hath appeared, bringing salvation to all men,** 12 **instructing us, to the intent that, denying ungodliness and worldly lusts, we should live soberly and righteously and godly in this present world;** 13 **looking for the blessed hope and appearing of the glory of the great God and our Saviour Jesus Christ;** 14 **who gave himself for us, that he might redeem us from all iniquity, and purify unto himself a people for his own possession, zealous of good works.**

As the opening 'for' indicates, Paul now points to the grace of God as the motivating power which enables believers to fulfil the ethical demands of the gospel [*vv* 1–10]. This is 'the first of the two Evangelical outbursts of that "spring of living water" in St. Paul's own heart which kept his life and teaching always green and fresh' (Humphreys) [cf 3.4–7].

For the grace of God hath appeared, bringing salvation to all men, Paul once again stresses the universal scope of the gospel by affirming that the grace of God has been revealed in the visible earthly appearance of Christ, the Sun of Righteousness, whose coming dispelled the darkness of our nature's night. The gospel is good news for all men, 'because, when God calls upon men universally to believe, he does not call upon them to believe that they are elected, or that Christ died for them in particular. He calls upon them to believe that Christ died for sin, for sinners, for the world . . . The atonement is not offered to an individual either as an elect man, or as a non-elect man; but as a man, and a sinner, simply' (Shedd). (See also comment on 1 *Tim* 1.1; 2.4, 6; 4.10).

instructing us, to the intent that, denying ungodliness and worldly lusts, we should live soberly and righteously and godly in this present world; The point of the whole paragraph is to underline the educative function of grace in transforming our present life, for the triumph of God's grace must be shown in the fruit of godly living [*Matt* 6.20; *Gal* 5.22, 23]. This 'categorical imperative' involves the once-for-all denial of the ungodliness and worldly lusts which characterized the old life, and the aorist participle may point to the baptismal vow as marking this decisive break with the past (see comment on 1 *Tim* 6.12, 13). The renunciation of the past makes way for the positive aim expressed by the three adverbs which follow. 'Sobriety keeps the house, and moderates the mind at home; righteousness looks forth and gives every man his due abroad; piety looks up to God and gives Him His right' (Taylor).

looking for the blessed hope and appearing of the glory of the great God and our Saviour Jesus Christ; The vivid expectation of Christ's return provides the grand incentive to such godly living. According to Paul, 'the blessed hope' of believers is not a secret event, for he immediately defines it as the visible appearance of the glory of Christ on the last day [1 Tim 6.14; cf Matt 16.27]. 'We can only conclude that the distinction between the Rapture of the Church and the Revelation of Christ is an inference which is nowhere asserted by the Word of God and not required by the terminology relating to the return of Christ . . . The parousia, the apocalypse, and the epiphany appear to be a single event. Any division of Christ's coming into two parts is an unproven inference' (G. E. Ladd, *The Blessed Hope*, p. 69). Since Christ's deity will then be manifested, Paul here fittingly adds 'great God' [cf Rom 9.5] to the title 'our Saviour' [1.4]. The passage provides us with a clear testimony to the proper deity of Christ, and it should occasion no surprise that Paul, 'who everywhere thinks and speaks of Christ as very God, should occasionally call him by the appropriate designation' (B. B. Warfield, *The Lord of Glory*, p. 255).

who gave himself for us, that he might redeem us from all iniquity, and purify unto himself a people for his own possession, zealous of good works. Paul next explains the twofold purpose of Christ's substitutionary sacrifice [Mark 10.45; Gal 1.4; 1 Tim 2.6]. 1. He gave himself to redeem us from all iniquity (or lawlessness), i.e., he 'paid the price to buy us free and take us away from all lawless living (ungodliness and worldly lusts, *v* 12)' (Lenski). 2. He gave himself to purify for himself 'a people for his own possession'. This last phrase recalls Exod 19.5 and its application to Christians identifies the Church as the New Israel [cf Gal 6.16; Phil 3.3; 1 Pet 2.9f.]. As our cleansing from the defilement of sin has qualified us for God's service, it is fitting that we should be 'zealous of good works'. 'Give God thine affections, else thine actions are still-born, and have no life in them. Now zeal is the extreme heat of all the affections, when they are seething or hissing hot, as the apostle's word is, Rom 12.11, when we love God and his people out of a pure heart fervently . . . Let God's love in the work of our redemption be duly pondered (as here), and it will fire us up to a holy contention in godliness' (Trapp).

*V*15: **These things speak and exhort and reprove with all authority. Let no man despise thee.**

Paul's closing words look back to 2.1. Titus must continue to give practical instruction in Christian living within the proper doctrinal setting. He is not only to speak these things, but is to exhort the people and reprove them as necessary, with all the authority of his divine commission. The final admonition appears to be addressed as much to the Cretans who will hear it read out as to Titus himself. He must not permit any man to 'despise' him. The original word literally means, 'to think round a thing; hence, to have thoughts beyond, to disregard'. He is so to conduct himself that no man will be able to evade the force of his words.

CHAPTER THREE

The Cretans must be taught to obey the civil authorities and to live at peace with all men [vv 1, 2]. These duties are enforced by the reminder of their former sinful state, and the unmerited kindness of God in the bestowal of that free salvation which made them the heirs of eternal life [vv 3–7]. The evidence of this great change is to be seen in the good works of believers, but useless speculations which engender strife are to be shunned [vv 8, 9]. After two warnings the obstinate heretics are to be avoided as being self-condemned [v 11]. When Artemas or Tychicus arrives, Paul requests Titus to join him at Nicopolis, and to give whatever help Zenas and Apollos may need on their journey. Such assistance befits believers, who are to show the fruits of their profession by serving others. After the customary salutations, Paul concludes with a benediction which embraces all the Christians in Crete [vv 12–15].

V1: **Put them in mind to be in subjection to rulers, to authorities, to be obedient, to be ready unto every good work, 2 to speak evil of no man, not to be contentious, to be gentle, showing all meekness toward all men.**

Titus must remind the unruly Cretans of their obligation to obey the civil authorities, and to be ready for any good work which will be of benefit to the community [*Rom* 13.1ff.; 1 *Tim* 2.2]. In contrast to their former mode of life [*v* 3], they are now to reflect the kindness of God in their conduct towards all men. On the negative side, they are not to revile any man, nor be contentious (this word literally means, 'non-fighters'). Positively, they are to be gentle or forbearing, willing to yield their rights to others, 'showing *all* meekness to *all* men'. Such meekness 'is an inwrought grace of the soul; and the exercises of it are first and chiefly towards God, when we accept his dealings with us without disputing . . . He that is meek indeed will know himself a sinner among sinners; or if there was One who could not know Himself such, yet He too bore a sinner's doom and endured therefore the contradiction of sinners [cf *Matt* 11.29: "I am meek and lowly of heart"]; and this knowledge of his own sin will teach him to endure meekly the provocations with which they may provoke him, and not to withdraw himself from the burdens which their sin may impose upon him [*Gal* 6.1; 2 *Tim* 2.25]' (R. C. Trench).

*V*3: **For we also once were foolish, disobedient, deceived, serving divers lusts and pleasures, living in malice and envy, hateful, hating one another.**

Paul's use of the plural 'we' shows that his statement is true of all believers including himself and Titus: We have good reason to manifest such meekness toward the unsaved when we remember that we were once like them ourselves [cf *Eph* 2.1–3]. A mournful proof of the depravity of human nature is provided by this sevenfold description of our former sinful state. At that time we also were: 1. 'foolish', without understanding through the blinding effect of sin upon the mind [*Eph* 4.18]; 2. 'disobedient', to both God and man, rebelling against the dictates of conscience and the constraints of the law; 3. 'deceived', made to wander from the true way through following the reasonings of unbelief; 4. 'serving divers lusts and pleasures', being dominated by the desire for self-gratification; 5. 'living in malice and envy', showing ill-will towards others and coveting what is theirs; 6. 'hateful', made detestable to others through the self-centredness of sin; 7. 'hating one another', for mutual hatred is the inevitable result of such sinful egocentricity.

*V*4: **But when the kindness of God our Saviour, and his love toward man, appeared, 5 not by works *done* in righteousness, which we did ourselves, but according to his mercy he saved us, through the washing of regeneration and renewing of the Holy Spirit, 6 which he poured out upon us richly, through Jesus Christ our Saviour; 7 that, being justified by his grace, we might be made heirs according to the hope of eternal life.**

The fourth of the Faithful sayings [*v* 8] ascribes the work of salvation entirely to God, and so focuses on the way in which that salvation is applied to sinners that many scholars think Paul is here quoting part of a baptismal creed or hymn, which faithfully echoes his own teaching. As Warfield well says, These sayings 'represent the form which his doctrinal expositions had taken as current coin in the churches, no longer merely Paul's teaching, though all of that, but the precious possessions of the people themselves, in which they were able to give back to him a response from their listening hearts' (The Way of Life' in *Faith and Life*, p. 394).

But when the kindness of God our Saviour, and his love toward man, appeared, 'But' marks the great change wrought in us by the action of God [*Eph* 2.4ff.]. It was when 'the kindness' of God and his 'love-toward-man' (our 'philanthropy') appeared in the first coming of Christ [2.11; 2 *Tim* 1.10], that he *saved us* through the renewing power of the Holy Spirit, and consequently we now gladly confess him to be God '*our Saviour*'!

not by works *done* in righteousness, which we did ourselves, The emphatic denial that man can contribute anything to his salvation is an essential element in Paul's gospel and in all authentic preaching [*Rom* 3.27, 28; 4.2–6; 9.11; *Gal* 2.16; *Eph* 2.9; 2 *Tim* 1.9]. For as Trapp pithily remarks, 'We that are bankrupts in Adam, would yet fain be doing, and think to be saved for a company of poor beggarly duties; as bankrupts will be trading again, though but for pins, etc.'.

but according to his mercy he saved us, through the washing of regeneration and renewing of the Holy Spirit, Having ruled out any thought of obtaining salvation by co-operating with God, this positive statement attributes our salvation solely to the mercy of God, which found expression in the sovereign bestowal of his regenerating grace [cf *Eph* 2.4, 5]. The actual application of the redemption wrought by Christ is the work of the Holy Spirit, who imparts new life to man in 'regeneration', and this 'renewal' (RSV) is the radical once-for-all change that makes him a new creature [2 *Cor* 5.17]. Since both these

TITUS, CHAPTER 3, VERSE 5

terms are used to explain how God saved us, there is no reference here to the progressive work of sanctification which does call for the active co-operation of believers [*Rom* 12.1, 2]. 'Washing' clearly has some reference to baptism, and this word was chosen because it could point to both the outward ordinance and the inner spiritual reality which that rite symbolized. Hence in the baptismal setting of this saying, believers 'confess that God has already saved them through the radical inner washing wrought by the Holy Spirit, a washing that may be spoken of as regeneration and renewal. And they do so at the time when they receive that which signifies that washing, even baptism' (George W. Knight, *The Faithful Sayings in the Pastoral Letters*, p. 111).

which he poured out upon us richly, through Jesus Christ our Saviour; Although 'he poured out' recalls the prophecy which received its primary fulfilment on the day of Pentecost (Joel 2.28ff.), the reference here is to the work of the Spirit in regeneration and conversion [*Rom* 5.5; 1 *Cor* 2.12; *Gal* 4.6; *Eph* 1.13]. This rich bestowal 'is expressly connected with the mediation of Christ, who as Saviour has opened the way for it, and Himself sends forth the Spirit as the fruit of His work on earth, and the token of its acceptance with the Father. So that the whole Trinity appears here as concurring in the blessed work of our salvation' (Fairbairn). [cf *Luke* 24.29; *Acts* 2.33].

that, being justified by his grace, we might be made heirs according to the hope of eternal life. This expresses the final purpose of God in the bestowal of the Spirit. It is that, having been justified by his grace (i.e. declared righteous 'through the redemption that is in

Christ Jesus', *Rom* 3.24; cf 2.14), we might at once become 'heirs' in accord with the sure hope of eternal life. 'The apostle is speaking not of the future, but of the present condition of believers. They *are* heirs of eternal life; but they are so in hope, not yet in actual possession; for *eternal life* in its full meaning is something future, *Rom* 6.22, 23' (Huther).

*V*8: **Faithful is the saying, and concerning these things I desire that thou affirm confidently, to the end that they who have believed God may be careful to maintain good works. These things are good and profitable unto men:**

In contrast to the dogmatism of ignorance [1 *Tim* 1.7], Titus knows the reality of the evangelical truths set forth in the preceding 'faithful saying' [*vv* 4–7]. Hence he is to affirm 'these things' with confidence, being convinced of their practical bearing on the conduct of believers. For a genuine experience of God's grace must be reflected in a life of gratitude [*Rom* 12.1ff.]. 'It is most significant and suggestive that the apostle held that good works were most certainly assured by a theology which gives special prominence to the free unmerited grace of God' (White).

*V*9: **but shun foolish questionings, and genealogies, and strifes, and fightings about the law; for they are unprofitable and vain.**

Titus must shun the foolish speculations and genealogies, which lead to disputes and quarrels about the law, for they are unprofitable and vain [see comment on 1.14 and 1 *Tim* 1.4]. He must teach the sound doctrine that promotes

godliness [1.1], and not emulate the folly of those who
had turned aside to matters which did not relate to the
truth of salvation. 'In teaching we are always to have
regard to usefulness so that all that is not conducive to
godliness may be excluded. There is no doubt that the
sophists in their ranting about things of no worth boasted
of them as highly worthy and useful to know, but Paul
does not admit any usefulness except in building up faith
and a holy life' (Calvin).

V 10: **A factious man after a first and second admonition refuse; 11 knowing that such a one is perverted,
and sinneth, being self-condemned.**

A 'factious' man here refers to an 'opinionative propa-
gandist who promotes dissension by his pertinacity'
(Simpson). If he still persists in his self-chosen opinions
after having been twice warned of his error, Titus must
have nothing more to do with him, 'recognizing that a
man of that sort has a distorted mind and stands self-
condemned in his sin' (NEB). For though he may not be
condemned by his own conscience, he is at least condemned by his own action. 'He is self-condemned because
his separation from the Church is due to his own acknowledged act. He cannot deny that his views are antagonistic
to those which he once accepted as true; he is condemned
by his former, and, as St. Paul would say, his more
enlightened self' (White).

V 12: **When I shall send Artemas unto thee, or Tychicus, give diligence to come unto me to Nicopolis:
for there I have determined to winter.**

In closing Paul informs Titus that he will send either Artemas (who is mentioned only here) or Tychicus [*Acts* 20.4; *Eph* 6.21; *Col* 4.7; *2 Tim* 4.12] to replace him in Crete, and when thus released instructs him to proceed to Nicopolis in Epirus (on the west coast of Achaia), where the apostle had decided to spend the winter.

*V*13: **Set forward Zenas the lawyer and Apollos on their journey diligently, that nothing be wanting unto them.** 14 **And let our** *people* **also learn to maintain good works for necessary uses, that they be not unfruitful.**

Paul next requests Titus to give Zenas and Apollos, who are evidently the bearers of this letter, whatever assistance they may need to continue on their journey. 'Those that labour in the Lord's work must have all necessary accommodations and encouragements. They must be set forth and brought forward on their journey and in their negotiations worthy of God, 3 *John* 6' (Trapp). This will also provide the Christians of Crete with an opportunity to learn how to help others in urgent need, so that they do not prove to be unfruitful professors. Nothing further is known of Zenas who was probably a Roman jurist, but Apollos is almost certainly the eloquent Alexandrian who preached at Corinth [*Acts* 18.24; 1 *Cor* 1.12, 16.12].

*V*15: **All that are with me salute thee. Salute them that love us in faith.**
     Grace be with you all.

As the workers with Paul join in sending their greetings to Titus, so Titus is to pass on these greetings to those who 'love us in faith', i.e. 'in the sphere of faith'. The brief benediction embraces all the Cretan believers, and this shows that Paul intended the whole church to hear his letter.

2 TIMOTHY

CHAPTER ONE

Paul affectionately greets Timothy, for whom he constantly prays, and longs to see, having received a reminder of his sincere faith which dwelt first in his grandmother and mother [vv 1–5]. He urges him to stir up the gift of God which is in him, and not to be ashamed of the testimony of the gospel, but to be ready to suffer for it by the power of God, who saved and called them both into his service (vv 6–10). It is due to his fidelity to the gospel that Paul is now a prisoner, but he is not ashamed, for he has entrusted himself to the Lord's safe-keeping [vv 11, 12]. Timothy must hold fast the sound teaching and guard the good deposit with the help of the Holy Spirit [vv 13, 14]. This appeal is enforced by the sad reminder of the general desertion of Paul's converts in Asia, and on the other hand by the bright example of the faithfulness shown by Onesiphorus [vv 15–18].

V 1: **Paul, an apostle of Christ Jesus through the will of God, according to the promise of the life which is in Christ Jesus, 2 to Timothy, my beloved child: Grace, mercy, peace, from God the Father and Christ Jesus our Lord.**

The opening salutation is very similar to that of the First Epistle to Timothy, but as Paul here calmly faces the last great crisis of his life, he reaffirms that he is an apostle of

Christ Jesus 'through the will of God in accordance with
the promise of life which is in Christ Jesus'. His apostleship
was the result of that promise, for 'had there been no such
promise there could have been no *divinely willed apostle* to
proclaim the promise' (Hendriksen). This is the promise
of everlasting life – beginning in grace and perfected in
glory – which is found in union with Christ Jesus [*v* 10;
1 *Tim* 4.8]. In addressing Timothy as 'my beloved child',
Paul expresses the fatherly affection he feels for his own
son in the faith, and thus sets the tone for this heartfelt
and deeply moving letter of farewell. The greeting is
identical with that given in 1 *Tim* 1.2 (see comment there).

V 3: **I thank God, whom I serve from my forefathers
in a pure conscience, how unceasing is my remembrance of thee in my supplications, night and day 4
longing to see thee, remembering thy tears, that I
may be filled with joy; 5 having been reminded of
the unfeigned faith that is in thee; which dwelt first
in thy grandmother Lois, and thy mother Eunice;
and, I am persuaded, in thee also.**

Instead of reflecting upon his own sad plight, Paul begins
in a spirit of gratitude to God. This is prompted by the
treasured memories he has of his beloved child and by
some recent reminder of Timothy's faith from without,
conveyed perhaps by letter or messenger. The apostle
affirms that he serves God with the same purity of
conscience which characterized the worship of his forefathers, because the faith he proclaimed was the true
fulfilment of Israel's ancestral hope [*Acts* 24.14–16). 'Paul
always maintained that the Gospel was the divinely
ordained sequel of Judaism; not a new religion, but the

fulfilment of "the promise made of God unto our fathers" [*Acts* 26.6]' (White). He assures Timothy that he constantly remembers him in his prayers 'night and day' [cf AV and 1 *Tim* 5.5], and as he recalls Timothy's tears at their last parting, he longs to see him again that he may be filled with joy. Whatever reminded Paul of Timothy's sincere faith in Christ naturally led him to think of the prior conversion of Timothy's grandmother Lois and his mother Eunice. This probably took place during Paul's first visit to Lystra [*Acts* 14.6], for when he returned Timothy's mother was already a believer [*Acts* 16.1]. Finally, by expressing his confidence in the genuineness of Timothy's faith, Paul provides the basis for the ensuing appeal, *viz.* that Timothy should bear a courageous testimony to the truth in the face of affliction.

*V*6: **For which cause I put thee in remembrance that thou stir up the gift of God, which is in thee through the laying on of my hands.**

It is because Paul knows the reality of Timothy's commitment that he urges him to keep stirring into flame the gift of God which is in him. The bestowal of this ministerial gift was symbolized through the laying on of the apostle's hands at his ordination. Although this was an act in which the elders also joined, Paul only mentions his own part in that service here, since he is stressing the significance of the spiritual bond in his personal relationship with Timothy (see comment on 1 *Tim* 4.14). The exhortation shows that the gift for service does not operate automatically, but requires the active co-operation of its recipient to keep it ablaze [cf 1 *Thess* 5.19]. Paul does not imply that Timothy had been failing in his duty, for his use of the present infinitive rather means that his 'child' is to continue to fan the flame as he had been doing. This clarion call for untiring zeal in God's service demands the constant attention of every Christian worker, for frail flesh is prone to the lassitude which allows spiritual ardour to burn very low.

V 7: **For God gave us not a spirit of fearfulness; but of power and love and discipline.**

What God gave to Paul and Timothy for the work of ministry was not a spirit of craven fear, 'but a spirit of power and love and sound judgment' (Bruce). These are the three graces which are especially needed as the storm clouds of persecution begin to loom large on Timothy's horizon [*v* 8]. 1. 'Power' is the divine dynamic which imparts the strength to work on, to endure adversity, and to die if need be; 2. 'Love' is the self-denying grace which banishes fear [1 *John* 4.18] and is ready to risk all to save the flock; 3. 'Sound judgment' ensures that power and love are exercised with wisdom, and thus provides an essential safeguard against the dangers of fanaticism.

V 8: **Be not ashamed therefore of the testimony of our Lord, nor of me his prisoner: but suffer hardship with the gospel according to the power of God;**

In view of this divine enduement [*v* 7], Timothy must never be ashamed to testify about our Lord, even though the witness to a crucified Messiah inevitably excited the enmity and scorn of the world. White points out that the construction used here forbids the supposition that Timothy had actually done what Paul warns him against

doing. It is a call to continued fidelity which urges
Timothy not to become ashamed rather than to stop being
ashamed. Paul also adds the touching appeal, 'nor of me
his prisoner', for though he insists that he is the *Lord's*
prisoner and not Caesar's [cf *Eph* 3.1], when an acknowledged leader is treated like a criminal his assistants are
automatically involved in the same disgrace. Instead of
yielding to such a feeling of shame, let Timothy join with
Paul in suffering for the gospel [cf NIV], according to the
power that God gives [*v* 7]. For the power given is always
commensurate to the sufferings to be endured [2 *Cor* 12.9,
10].

*V*9: **who saved us, and called us with a holy calling,
not according to our works, but according to his
own purpose and grace, which was given us in Christ
Jesus before times eternal, 10 but hath now been
manifested by the appearing of our Saviour Christ
Jesus, who abolished death, and brought life and
immortality to light through the gospel,**

Theodore of Mopsuestia (c. 350–428) gives well the con-
necting thought which carries Paul here 'from his appeal
for boldness into another of his exulting Gospel anthems.
"Take," he says in effect, "take great pains, bear long
pains – for a gift so great, so age-long"' (cited by Humphreys).

who saved us, and called us with a holy calling, Since
our salvation is wholly of God, which he accomplished
without our aid, his almighty power is sufficient to sustain
us throughout every crisis of life [4.18]. And as we are
called with a holy calling, we must draw on that power to

live as befits the free-born citizens of heaven [1 *Cor* 1.2; *Phil* 2.12, 13; 3.20].

not according to our works, but according to his own purpose and grace, As in *Titus* 3.5ff., Paul inserts a characteristic disclaimer of man's merit, and emphasizes that our salvation is due solely to *God's own* sovereign purpose and grace. If we had merited the gospel, 'it had been hard to suffer for it; but our salvation by it is of free grace, and not according to our works, and therefore we must not think much to suffer for it' (Matthew Henry).

which was given us in Christ Jesus before times eternal, 'Before we existed, it was given to us, the Mediator even then receiving it' (Bengel). Thus our temporal trials, however severe they may be, are put into their proper perspective by the certainty of God's electing grace in Christ Jesus [cf *Eph* 1.4].

but hath now been manifested by the appearing of our Saviour Christ Jesus, Although the term 'appearing' is elsewhere used of Christ's return in glory, it here refers to the glorious dawning of God's eternal purpose of grace, which was embodied and made effective through the coming in the flesh of our Saviour.

who abolished death, and brought life and immortality to light through the gospel, Through his redemptive travail Christ has broken the power of death [*Heb* 2.14], and brought 'life' and 'immortality' to light. The believer's present experience of new 'life' in Christ will be consummated in the 'immortality' or incorruptibility of the resurrection body [1 *Cor* 15.53–57; *Phil* 3.21]. It is by means of the gospel that this revelation is made effective, 'for it is the power of God unto salvation' [*Rom* 1.16].

*V*11: **whereunto I was appointed a preacher, and an apostle, and a teacher.**

The mention of the word 'gospel' leads Paul to state his own relation to it. It is for this gospel that he was appointed a herald, and an apostle, and a teacher (see note on 1 *Tim* 2.7). So conscious was he of the great honour thus bestowed upon him that he could feel no shame in suffering for the gospel [*v* 12].

*V*12: **For which cause I suffer also these things: yet I am not ashamed; for I know him whom I have believed, and I am persuaded that he is able to guard that which I have committed unto him against that day.**

The phrase 'also these things' marks the climax in Paul's long career of suffering, since he was now facing the prospect of being executed as a criminal. Yet he is not ashamed to be found in such straits, 'for I know him whom I have believed', i.e. the Saviour who triumphed over death and brought to light 'life and immortality' [*v* 10]. Hence Paul is convinced that Christ is able to guard that which he has deposited with Him until that day [4.8]. In other words, he is assured of Christ's ability to save and keep him to the very end. The alternative view takes 'the deposit' to be the gospel entrusted to Paul [cf RSV, NEB], on the ground that it harmonizes with Paul's charge to Timothy in verse 14. Although this neatly deals with a difficulty, the intensely personal nature of Paul's affirma-

tion of faith may be said to favour the traditional interpretation adopted above.

*V*13: **Hold the pattern of sound words which thou
hast heard from me, in faith and love which is in
Christ Jesus.**

In resuming his advice to Timothy [*vv* 6–8], Paul next
urges him to remain true to the 'pattern' or 'model' (rather
in the sense of *standard*: Arndt-Gingrich) set by his own
teaching. In contrast to the diseased words peddled by
false teachers, Timothy's ministry must be firmly based
upon the 'healthy' words of the apostle's doctrine (see
comment on I *Tim* 1.10). But this must be done in that
spirit of faith and love, which is the fruit of living in union
with Christ Jesus. For without the enlivening presence of
faith and love even the purest teaching is bound to degener-
ate into a dead orthodoxy.

*V*14: **That good thing which was committed unto *thee*
guard through the Holy Spirit which dwelleth in us.**

'That good deposit' (ASV margin) is the gospel message
committed to Timothy, which he is to guard by the power
of the Holy Spirit. This means he must rely upon the help
of the Holy Spirit, who indwells all believers, 'and more
particularly assisteth the ministers of the gospel. We can
neither keep our minds sound in the faith, as to the
doctrine of it, nor our souls steady in the exercises of faith
or love, without the assistance of the Holy Spirit' (Poole).

*V*15: **This thou knowest, that all that are in Asia**

turned away from me; of whom are Phygelus and Hermogenes.

As an incentive to fidelity, Paul reminds Timothy of some notable examples of disloyalty and loyalty [*vv* 15–18]. Clearly 'turned away from *me*' cannot refer to apostasy, but presumably points to the moment of the apostle's re-arrest when he was deserted by the Christians of Asia, who seem to have been influenced by Phygelus and Hermogenes. 'These two are named because they were the most conspicuous in their unfaithfulness to the apostle' (Huther).

V 16: **The Lord grant mercy unto the house of Onesiphorus: for he oft refreshed me, and was not ashamed of my chain; 17 but, when he was in Rome, he sought me diligently, and found me 18 (the Lord grant unto him to find mercy of the Lord in that day); and in how many things he ministered at Ephesus, thou knowest very well.**

In contrast to the desertion of the majority, Onesiphorus (which means 'profit-bringer') had lived up to his name by ministering to Paul's needs in prison. He was not ashamed to be associated with a chained apostle, and diligently searched the prisons of Rome until he found him. As the grateful recipient of this mercy, Paul prays that the Lord may show mercy to the household of Onesiphorus [*Matt* 5.7], and that the Lord (Christ) will grant him to find mercy from the Lord (God) on judgment day. Moreover, this man's ministry to the imprisoned apostle was but the climax of his service, for Timothy knows very well how much valuable assistance he had rendered to the Christians at Ephesus. Those who wish to find a scriptural warrant for prayers for the dead assume that Paul's prayer for the household of Onesiphorus [cf 4.19] must mean that he was now dead. But it is more likely that Onesiphorus was separated from his family by distance rather than by death, and such a prayer would be entirely natural if he were still with Paul in Rome or on his way home.

CHAPTER TWO

Paul bids Timothy to be strong, and to ensure that the apostolic tradition is preserved through a succession of faithful teachers [vv 1–2]. He is to suffer hardship as a good soldier of Christ, because the facts of the gospel and the experience of the apostle prove that the endurance of such suffering is the necessary prelude to reigning with Christ in glory [vv 3–13]. In training others Timothy must warn them against engaging in useless word-battles which greatly hinder those who listen. As to himself, he must strive after God's approval as a workman who correctly interprets the word of truth [vv 14, 15]. He is to avoid the vain disputing that promotes ungodliness, and may even overthrow the faith of some, and must remember that the foundation of God stands secure, for the Lord knows those who are his [vv 16–19]. As a purified vessel is made fit for honourable use, so Timothy should see that his profession is matched by his practice. He must shun foolish controversies, and as the Lord's servant must show gentleness when dealing with his opponents in the hope of leading them to a change of heart and freeing them from the devil's clutches [vv 20–26].

V 1: **Thou therefore, my child, be strengthened in the grace that is in Christ Jesus.**

This emphatic appeal is based on Timothy's filial relation

to Paul. As a son bears the likeness of his father, so Timothy is to exhibit his spiritual kinship with the apostle by his continued fidelity to the gospel. He cannot do this in his own strength, but only as he is inwardly strengthened by means of the grace that is in Christ Jesus [*Eph* 6.10]. 'Weak grace may evidence pardon of sin; but it is strong grace that can overcome the temptations of Satan, 1 John 2.12, 14, and bear up the heart in strong consolation. The blessing upon man in the first creation was, "Increase and multiply"; in the second, "Grow in grace, be strong", &c.' (Trapp).

*V*2: **And the things which thou hast heard from me among many witnesses, the same commit thou to faithful men, who shall be able to teach others also.**

Those same gospel truths which Timothy had heard Paul proclaim among many witnesses over the years, he must now entrust to faithful men who will be competent to teach others also. The apostle does not speak of secret doctrines privately imparted to Timothy, but clearly refers to the truths which he preached throughout his public ministry. 'This is the true apostolic succession of the ministry: not an uninterrupted line of hands laid on which extends back to the apostles themselves so that all ordinations which are not in that line are null and void; but a succession of true apostolic doctrine, the deposit of what we still hear from Paul in his writings, this held by us in faithful hearts with competency to teach others these same things. The apostle did not evidently expect the future teachers of the church to produce new or different teaching. The gospel is changeless in all ages' (Lenski).

*V*3: **Suffer hardship with *me*, as a good soldier of Christ Jesus. 4 No soldier on service entangleth himself in the affairs of *this* life; that he may please him who enrolled him as a soldier.**

Endure hardship with us (NIV) Since the ministerial calling places Timothy in the front line of the battle, he must be willing to endure hardship along with his comrades, as a good soldier of Christ Jesus. As Calvin notes, this warfare does not consist in inflicting evil upon others, and so the stress lies not on the offensive capacities of the soldier, but on his iron discipline in facing the onslaught of the enemy. Such discipline is the result of his total commitment, for no soldier on active service allows himself to become entangled in the affairs of civilian life, because his one aim is to satisfy the officer who enlisted him. The issue here is not that of pay (as in 1 *Cor* 9.7), 'but of a radical turning aside from all the cheerful or sad demands of life and a turning to full readiness in relation to Christ' (C. Maurer, *TDNT*, Vol. VI, p. 641).

*V*5: **And if also a man contend in the games, he is not crowned, except he have contended lawfully.**

Paul's second image is drawn from the Greek games, and his point is that a professional athlete is not rewarded with 'the victor's crown unless he competes according to the rules' (NIV). This would include both the preliminary training and the regulations governing the race itself. 'As applied to the Christian minister the training is that of 1 *Tim* 4.7, the regulations those of the law of Christ, especially those laid down here in verses 10–12' (Lock).

*V*6: **The husbandman that laboureth must be the first to partake of the fruits.**

The truth set forth in this third illustration is that the farmer's hard work entitles him to the first share of the crop. Hence ministers who toil long and hard in God's service will be the first to rejoice in seeing the fruits of their labours safely harvested. 'It is the man who has bathed himself in sweat to secure a harvest who has the premier title to its produce. Labour expended on an object renders it our own' (Simpson). Thus, when taken together, these three metaphors show that the ministry of the gospel demands: 1. the whole-hearted devotion of the soldier; 2. the self-discipline of the athlete; 3. the wearisome toil of the farmer.

*V*7: **Consider what I say; for the Lord shall give thee understanding in all things.**

If Timothy will reflect on the meaning of what Paul has just said, he will see that he must suffer his share of hardship before he can enjoy the reward which is implied in each of the preceding figures (the victory after battle; the prize after the race; the harvest after much labour). Let Timothy duly ponder the apostle's teaching, and the Lord will give him the enlightenment he needs. So we cannot expect to grasp the meaning of Scripture unless we give our minds to it, but true spiritual understanding is always the Lord's gift to us.

*V*8: **Remember Jesus Christ, risen from the dead, of the seed of David, according to my gospel:**

If it be asked why Paul here introduces this pregnant statement of the central facts of the gospel entrusted to him, the answer cannot lie in the need to remind Timothy of the truth of the doctrine, but rather in its application to the hardships he must endure as the preacher of a faith outlawed by men. Hence it should be seen as a call to follow the path marked out by the Saviour who suffered the agonies of the cross before he was crowned with glory and honour. 'Remember it for thine encouragement; that Christ, for a reward of his sufferings, was both raised and exalted, Phil. 2.9' (Trapp). Timothy will be strengthened for the conflict as he keeps in mind the raised and reigning heir of David's line, Jesus Christ, with whom we shall also live and reign in glory [*vv* 11, 12].

*V*9: **wherein I suffer hardship unto bonds, as a malefactor; but the word of God is not bound.**

It is for this gospel that Paul is suffering 'even to the point of being chained like a criminal' (NIV). The strength of his language indicates how deeply he felt the shame and degradation of his imprisonment, but he rejoices in the fact that the word of God is not chained! 'Persecuting powers may silence ministers and restrain them, but they cannot hinder the operation of the word of God upon men's hearts and consciences; that cannot be bound by any human force' (Matthew Henry).

*V*10: **Therefore I endure all things for the elect's sake, that they also may obtain the salvation which is in Christ Jesus with eternal glory.**

Because Paul knows that his sufferings promote the advance of the gospel, he willingly endures all things for the sake of 'the elect', i.e. those whom God has predestined and chosen for salvation [*Rom* 8.33; *Col* 3.12; *Titus* 1.1]. His sufferings thus have an evangelistic purpose: it is that the elect 'also' (they as well as he) may obtain the salvation which is 'in Christ Jesus'. He here views his apostolic vocation in the light of God's electing grace, because his sufferings could never help to save those who were not so chosen [cf *Col* 1.24: 'for his body's sake, which is the church']. On the other hand, the investment of the elect 'with eternal glory' requires the use of the means ordained by God to achieve that end [cf 2 *Thess* 2.13, 14]. As an instrument of God's saving purpose, the apostle Paul knew that his testimony in preaching, writing, and suffering 'was for all countries and for all time; and the elect of this present age are in many ways reaping the benefit of his self-denying and devoted labours' (Fairbairn).

*V*11: **Faithful is the saying: For if we died with him, we shall also live with him: 12 if we endure, we shall also reign with him: if we shall deny him, he also will deny us: 13 if we are faithless, he abideth faithful; for he cannot deny himself.**

The last of the five faithful sayings in the Pastorals is another fragment of an early Christian hymn, which some scholars have seen as a 'Hymn to Martyrdom', but the language used suggests that it rather belongs to a baptismal setting.

For if we died with him, we shall also live with

him: These words clearly recall *Rom* 6.8, and point to baptism as the decisive past-event which marked the end of the old life and the beginning of the new [*Rom* 6.3, 4]. If we died with Christ in his once-for-all death to sin [*Rom* 6.10], then we shall also certainly live with him [*Rom* 6.4–6].

if we endure, we shall also reign with him: Between our past death and future hope, there lies our present responsibility, and this accounts for the omission of the preposition 'with him' from the verb 'endure' [cf *Rom* 8.17]. If we continue to endure to the end of our earthly course, then we shall also reign with him in glory. Thus reigning *with* Christ is the reward promised to those who now suffer *for* him.

if we shall deny him, he also will deny us: But another dreadful possibility has to be faced. If we shall perchance disown Christ, then he too will disown us [*Matt* 10.33]. In contrast to the comfort of the first two lines, we have here a warning against the dire consequences of apostasy. It is by heeding such warnings that the elect are brought safely to heaven [*Heb* 6.9].

if we are faithless, he abideth faithful; for he cannot deny himself. But as not every act of unfaithfulness amounts to outright apostasy, the fourth line brings a final word of comfort to believers who are troubled by their frequent failure to live up to their profession. 'What if we do not always remain steadfast? Does our every "denial" cause Christ to deny us for ever? No, if we are faithless, he abides faithful, for he cannot deny himself . . . The Christ with whom we have died remains faithful to us, not in the final analysis because of our faithfulness, but because he cannot deny himself' (George W. Knight, *The Faithful Sayings in the Pastoral Letters*, p. 136). [cf *Rom* 3.3].

V14: **Of these things put them in remembrance, charging *them* in the sight of the Lord, that they strive not about words, to no profit, to the subverting of them that hear.**

This verse sets forth Timothy's duty as a trainer of other teachers, the 'faithful men' mentioned in verse 2. The charge which Paul had laid on him must also be passed on to them. For they need to be reminded that the whole object of their ministry is to benefit their hearers, and not to upset their faith! Hence Timothy must warn them before God not to engage in useless word-battles, as this only 'subverts' (literally: turns upside down) those they should be building up.

V15: **Give diligence to present thyself approved unto God, a workman that needeth not to be ashamed, handling aright the word of truth.**

Turning back to Timothy, Paul urges him to make every effort to present himself to God as one approved. He is to be like a workman who has no need to be ashamed of the quality of his work. And for Timothy this entails 'handling aright the word of truth'. According to Arndt-Gingrich, the idea conveyed by the use of the word in *Prov* 3.6 and 11.5 is that of cutting a straight road through a forest or difficult country so that the traveller may go directly to his destination. This suggests that it here means: 'guide the word of truth along a straight path (like a road that goes straight to its goal), without being turned aside by wordy debates or impious talk'.

V16: **But shun profane babblings: for they will proceed further in ungodliness, 17 and their word will eat as doth a gangrene: of whom is Hymenaeus and Philetus; 18 men who concerning the truth have erred, saying that the resurrection is past already, and overthrow the faith of some.**

Timothy must avoid the godless chatter of the false teachers whose only 'progress' is towards even more ungodliness! For the effect of their teaching upon the church is like the spreading of a gangrenous growth which eats into the flesh. Of these errorists, Paul specially mentions Hymenaeus [1 *Tim* 1.20] and Philetus, who had gone astray from the truth by teaching that the resurrection had already taken place, and this was upsetting the faith of some. Like the sceptics in Corinth, they rejected the future resurrection of the body, presumably on the ground that they had already experienced the resurrection of the soul in baptism [*Rom* 6.4; *Col* 2.12]. 'It was altogether a spiritual thing in their account, a quickening merely of the soul's activities to newness of life; and thus, by their excess in spiritualizing, they loosened the very foundations of the Christian system; for the position they assumed involved by necessary inference the denial of Christ's resurrection, and the saving efficacy of His death [1 *Cor* 15.12–19]' (Fairbairn).

V19: **Howbeit the firm foundation of God standeth, having this seal, The Lord knoweth them that are**

his: and, Let every one that nameth the name of the Lord depart from unrighteousness.

But despite the false teachers and their deluded followers, Paul assures Timothy that God's firm foundation still stands secure – i.e. the true church remains unmoved by such errors [cf 1 *Tim* 3.15] – because its inviolability is guaranteed by the divine seal. This seal bears two inscriptions which recall the abortive rebellion of Korah, Dathan, and Abiram against Moses, the true servant of the Lord. After expressing confidence in the Lord's vindication of his leadership, Moses exhorts the people to depart from the tents of these wicked men [*Num* 16.5, 26]. As applied to the present crisis, the first inscription underlines the eternal security of the church, while the second stresses the purity which is required to provide public proof of its secret election. These are but two sides of the same coin, for God's election is always to holiness [*Eph* 1.4]. Hence the Lord's true servants will show that they are really known of God by forsaking wickedness, which in this context refers to the false teaching that is both dishonouring to God and ruinous to men.

*V*20: **Now in a great house there are not only vessels of gold and of silver, but also of wood and of earth; and some unto honour, and some unto dishonour. 21 If a man therefore purge himself from these, he shall be a vessel unto honour, sanctified, meet for the master's use, prepared unto every good work.**

Paul explains the mixed state of the church in the gospel age by another metaphor. In a great house there are many vessels with functions which vary according to their worth. Those of gold and silver are set aside for honourable use, but those of wood and earthenware are used for menial purposes and are discarded after having served their purpose. So the presence of false teachers in the church is only a temporary phenomenon, which serves to warn the faithful of the perils of apostasy. Paul therefore advises Timothy to cleanse himself 'from these', i.e. he is to separate himself from men like Hymenaeus and Philetus [*v* 17]. In this way he will prove himself to be a vessel 'unto honour', for in having been thus set apart for holy service, he is now useful to Christ his Master, and is permanently prepared for every good work.

*V*22: **But flee youthful lusts, and follow after righteousness, faith, love, peace, with them that call on the Lord out of a pure heart.**

As Timothy was still a young man [see 1 *Tim* 4.12], Paul bids him flee from all youthful desires (e.g. impatience, conceit, dogmatism, contentiousness, as well as sexual lust) which are inconsistent with the positive virtues he must pursue, namely, righteousness, faith, love, and peace. For in so doing he will keep company with those who 'call on the Lord out of a pure heart', which clearly implies that the pastor must not be less holy than his flock! The exhortation thus shows that character is more important than charisma. As Fairbairn well says, 'A sound moral condition is above all things essential to fitness for effective ministerial service in the divine kingdom. Other things may more or less be helpful, but this is indispensable'.

*V*23: **But foolish and ignorant questionings refuse, knowing that they gender strifes.**

Paul again warns Timothy not to have anything to do with the foolish and uninstructed speculations of the false teachers [cf 1 *Tim* 1.4; 4.7]. Parry points out that the second adjective is a very shrewd hit, for it denies the exact quality on which such teachers would pride themselves. 'These speculations show a half-educated mind, untrained to see the real points at issue and the true importance of things'. If Timothy appeared to endorse these futile questionings, believers would be distracted from the verities of the faith and become engaged in strifes which would divide and destroy the church.

*V*24: **And the Lord's servant must not strive, but be gentle towards all, apt to teach, forbearing,** 25 **in meekness correcting them that oppose themselves; if peradventure God may give them repentance unto the knowledge of the truth,** 26 **and they may recover themselves out of the snare of the devil, having been taken captive by him unto his will.**

Timothy is here further advised that the Lord's servant, like his supreme Exemplar [*Matt* 12.19], must not strive. He must not delight in controversy, but is to be kind to all, showing skill in teaching, and 'bearing evil without resentment' (Arndt-Gingrich). '*Gentle* unto all men, so he will be *apt to teach*; *forbearing* towards opponents, so he will be able to *correct*' (Bengel). For there is always the possibility that God may give them the grace of repentance, thus enabling them to turn from their errors and leading them into the full knowledge of the truth, which they now falsely claimed to possess. Only such a divinely given change of heart can arouse them from the stupefaction of their sinful state, so that they can escape from the snare of the devil, in which they were held captive to do his will. This means that sinners are so drugged by the devil's potions that they mistake bondage for freedom, and remain his willing slaves until they are brought to their senses by the power of God's grace.

CHAPTER THREE

Paul predicts that the last days will be marked by unparalleled moral decadence when a form of godliness will be professed but its power denied. Those who already exhibit such characteristics must be avoided by Timothy, for their deception of weak-minded women and their opposition to the truth shows them to be men of counterfeit faith, whose folly will become evident to all [vv 1–9]. After a reminder of his own teaching and the sufferings he endured for the gospel, Paul urges Timothy to show the same faithfulness in the face of persecution [vv 10–12]. As deceivers wax worse, Timothy is to abide in the truths he had learned, being assured that the sacred writings which he had known from childhood were able to make him wise unto salvation through faith in Christ. All Scripture is inspired by God, and is therefore able to equip the man of God for all his work [vv 13–17].

*V*1: **But know this, that in the last days grievous times shall come.**

Since such opposition to the truth is characteristic of this present evil age, Timothy must neither be surprised nor dismayed by it, but is to recognize that the church will face terrible times 'in the last days' before Christ's return [2 *Pet* 3.3; *Jude* 18]. For as the end approaches there will be a fearful increase in wickedness, when evil men will abound in the same vices which have already appeared in those whom Timothy is now to avoid [vv 2–5, 13; 4.3, 4]. 'The revelations Paul has received are God's advance warnings to fortify his ministers and their churches. Paul, approaching his end, is passing these warnings on' (Lenski).

V2: **For men shall be lovers of self, lovers of money, boastful, haughty, railers, disobedient to parents, unthankful, unholy, 3 without natural, affection, implacable, slanderers, without self-control, fierce, no lovers of good, 4 traitors, headstrong, puffed up, lovers of pleasure rather than lovers of God;**

'Lovers of self, lovers of money' provides the key to this list of vices, for moral corruption is the inevitable consequence of the misdirected love which seeks self-gratification through the things that money can buy [1 *Tim* 6.10], and thus makes men 'lovers of pleasure rather than lovers of God'. This self-centredness naturally leads to the self-assertiveness that is 'boastful, proud, abusive' (NIV). The megalomania which enthrones self is also devoid of any sense of natural decency, for it is unfilial, unthankful, unholy, unloving, and unforgiving! In the remaining seven terms the aggressive character of such egoism comes strongly to the fore. It is given to false accusation, and will go to any lengths to satisfy its lusts. Its brutality is not tempered by any love of the good, while its treacherous and reckless conduct is inspired by an overweening conceit.

V5: **holding a form of godliness, but having denied the power thereof: from these also turn away.**

[151]

In his final charge Paul clearly has the Ephesian Judaists in mind. He accuses them of hypocrisy in holding to the outward semblance of godliness, when their actions prove that they are strangers to the regenerating power of the gospel, which they have in effect totally denied. And from these false teachers Timothy is to turn away.

*V*6: **For of these are they that creep into houses, and take captive silly women laden with sins, led away by divers lusts, 7 ever learning, and never able to come to the knowledge of the truth.**

Men of this kind propagate their errors by worming their way into houses and misleading weak-minded women, burdened with sins and led on by various desires, who are always learning but never able to reach a knowledge of the truth [see comment on 1 *Tim* 2.4]. As Satan's strategy was first to deceive Eve, so heretical teachers have often chosen to spread their falsehoods by the same method. Impressionable women, oppressed by feelings of guilt, are eager to try any quack remedy which does not require them to abandon their sins. Hence their morbid curiosity in religious novelties prevents them from coming to a realization of the truth.

*V*8: **And even as Jannes and Jambres withstood Moses, so do these also withstand the truth; men corrupted in mind, reprobate concerning the faith.**

Just as Jannes and Jambres opposed God's spokesman before Pharaoh, so do these men oppose the truth of the gospel. This is a shrewd shaft against the sectaries. Since they are so fond of Jewish myths and genealogies, let them recall how the Egyptian magicians who opposed Moses were confounded [*Exod* 7.11; 9.11]. Although their names are not given in the Old Testament record, they were preserved by Jewish tradition, with which Paul was familiar through his rabbinical training under Gamaliel [*Acts* 22.3]. The apostle here brands these errorists as men whose minds have been hopelessly corrupted, and who are therefore utterly rejected so far as the faith is concerned. As the organ by which the truth is received is corrupt, they are disqualified, for they cannot even accept the doctrines of the gospel let alone teach them to others.

*V*9: **But they shall proceed no further: for their folly shall be evident unto all men, as theirs also came to be.**

But Timothy need not fear that these men will be any more successful than Jannes and Jambres were in opposing the truth. For despite the threat posed by the heretics, their progress is more apparent than real, and the hollowness of their pretensions will soon be revealed. 'Truth *must* prevail in the end, and imposture cannot permanently deceive' (Bernard).

*V*10: **But thou didst follow my teaching, conduct, purpose, faith, longsuffering, love, patience,** 11 **persecutions, sufferings; what things befell me at Antioch, at Iconium, at Lystra; what persecutions I endured: and out of them all the Lord delivered me.**

But in contrast to the teachers of error, Timothy is fully qualified to teach the true faith, having closely followed the steps of his master and observed the example thus set both in doctrine and life. Paul describes the content of this course of instruction in a list of nine items. 'My teaching' is naturally placed first and covers what the apostle taught and the way he taught it, while 'conduct' shows that his manner of life was perfectly consistent with the truth he confessed. Paul was sustained in his 'purpose', his steadfast resolve to devote his life to the furtherance of the gospel, by his own 'faith' in God's word. His 'long-suffering' enabled him to persevere in his labours until the fruit appeared, and this was made possible by his outgoing 'love' for the lost. 'Patience, persecutions, sufferings' refer to what Paul willingly suffered for the sake of the gospel, and he instances what befell him at Pisidian Antioch, Iconium, and Lystra because these events must have made a profound impression upon the young Timothy [cf *Acts* 16.1f with 13.50; 14.2, 5, 19]. As Paul looks back at the persecutions he endured, he adds 'yet out of them all the Lord rescued me' in order to teach Timothy to rely upon the same help in similar straits. 'The Lord ever rescues his people, frequently *from* death, sometimes *by means of* death. Either way, nothing ever separates them from his love' [*Rom* 8.38, 39] (Hendriksen).

V 12: **Yea, and all that would live godly in Christ Jesus shall suffer persecution.**

Moreover, Paul's experience was not exceptional, for persecution is the lot of all who intend to live a godly life in union with Christ Jesus [cf *Acts* 14.22]. The world's hostility to the gospel will not always be of the same intensity, but in so far as it 'retains its native character, those who are bent on leading in it lives of piety shall have to meet persecution' (Fairbairn). [*John* 16.33; 1 *John* 3.13]

*V*13: **But evil men and imposters shall wax worse and worse, deceiving and being deceived.**

But though untouched by such distress, evil men and imposters of the kind already mentioned [*vv* 2–9] will progress from bad to worse, deceiving and being deceived. As teachers their success will be limited [*v* 9], but they will increase in wickedness through becoming the dupes of their self-chosen errors. For those who set out to deceive others are themselves brought under the enslaving power of the same delusion.

*V*14: **But abide thou in the things which thou hast learned and hast been assured of, knowing of whom thou hast learned them;**

Paul again makes an emphatic contrast between Timothy's sure grounding in the truth and the deceptive delusions of the false teachers [cf *v* 10]: 'But as for you, continue in what you have learned, and have become convinced of, because you know those from whom you learned it' (NIV). Timothy was certain of the truth of what he had learned, because the content of that teaching was closely reflected in the character of his teachers. As Paul's son in the faith, Timothy obviously owed most to the apostle himself, but the next verse shows that the primary reference is to the formative influence exercised upon Timothy by his mother and grandmother [1.5].

*V*15: **and that from a babe thou hast known the sacred**

writings which are able to make thee wise unto salvation through faith which is in Christ Jesus.

It is due to the fidelity of these teachers that Timothy's knowledge of the Old Testament Scriptures stretches back to his earliest years. Paul affirms that the 'sacred' writings, in contrast to all those of purely human origin, are uniquely able to give the wisdom that leads to salvation. As a guide to salvation, the Old Testament is not a revelation that is complete in itself, for it points forward to Christ as the fulfiller of all its promises. Hence Paul's qualifying phrase is directed against the 'vain jangling' to which the Scriptures were being subjected by those who had rejected the key to their correct interpretation [*Luke* 24.44ff]. The endless genealogies and Jewish myths 'on which these letters pour contempt, were the stock-in-trade of men versed in the allegorical method, and who practised a puerile and speculative treatment of inspired Scripture. So the occasion has come to formulate the doctrine of inspiration implicit throughout St. Paul's teaching [see specially *Rom* 15.4 and 1 *Cor* 10.11]. That doctrine exhibits in the words "through faith that is in Christ Jesus" its specially Pauline stamp and character' (Findlay).

V 16: **Every scripture inspired of God** *is* **also profitable for teaching, for reproof, for correction, for instruction which is in righteousness:**

This translation is open to serious objection in that it suggests there may be other scriptures which are not inspired by God. Since the sentence. lacks a main verb, 'is' has to be supplied by the translators, but it is more natural to insert this immediately after the subject, 'scripture'.

The same construction is found in 1 *Tim* 4.4, which, Simpson drily notes, no one translates: 'every good creature of God is also not one of them to be rejected'! Moreover, the absence of the article does not invariably require the rendering 'every', for it would be equally foolish to translate *Acts* 2.36 as 'every house of Israel' instead of 'all (the) house of Israel' [cf *Eph* 2.21; 3.15]. Paul's thought here is accurately conveyed by the AV, but the NIV gives the literal meaning of his words: **All Scripture is God-breathed.** As Warfield was at pains to point out, the Greek term does not mean that God inspired ('breathed into') the Scripture or its human authors, but that Scripture is the product of divine spiration ('breathed out by God'). 'What it affirms is that the Scriptures owe their origin to an activity of God the Holy Ghost and are in the highest and truest sense His creation. It is on this foundation of Divine origin that all the high attributes of Scripture are built' (*The Inspiration and Authority of the Bible*, p. 296).

and profitable for teaching, for reproof, for correction, and for training in righteousness, (RSV) It is precisely because all Scripture is God-breathed that it is so universally profitable. The Word of God provides a complete guide to doctrine and practice. As to doctrine, it is profitable for teaching the truth and for refuting all falsehood. As to practice, it is profitable for restoring the fallen and for training in all righteous living.

*V*17: **that the man of God may be complete, furnished completely unto every good work.**

God's purpose in thus providing the Scripture is that the

man of God may be completely equipped for every good work. Although in this context 'the man of God' appears to refer to the Christian leader, the title may also be fitly applied to every believer [see comment on 1 *Tim* 6.11]. The Scripture 'is so full a direction, that Christians need not go down to the Philistines to whet their tools, nor be beholden to unwritten traditions, or to the writings of pagan philosophers, for directions what to do, how to worship God, or manage any part of their conversation, either as to their general calling, or as to their particular relations' (Poole).

CHAPTER FOUR

In his final charge to Timothy, Paul presses him to preach the Word and to fulfil his ministry, even though some may prefer the myths of men to the truth of God [vv 1–5]. As for Paul, the contest is over, and he now awaits the crown which the Lord will also give to all who have set their hearts on his appearing [vv 6–8]. Timothy is to come as soon as he can, bringing Mark with him, and also Paul's cloak, books, and parchments · [vv 9–13]. He is also to be on his guard against Alexander the coppersmith who did Paul much harm [vv 14, 15]. All deserted Paul at his first defence, but the Lord enabled him to proclaim the message and delivered him from the lion's mouth [vv 16, 17]. And he is confident that the Lord will deliver him from every evil work and bring him safely to his heavenly kingdom [v 18]. After various greetings, and a last word of entreaty, the letter ends with a prayer and the benediction [vv 19–22].

V1: **I charge *thee* in the sight of God, and of Christ Jesus, who shall judge the living and the dead, and by his appearing and his kingdom: 2 preach the word; be urgent in season, out of season; reprove, rebuke, exhort, with all longsuffering and teaching.**

In this paragraph the Epistle reaches its climax as Paul solemnly adjures Timothy to remain faithful to his charge

now that the time of his own departure is at hand [*vv*
1–8]. Since Timothy must one day give an account of his
stewardship, Paul lays this mandate upon him in the
presence of God and of Christ Jesus, who shall judge the
living and the dead [*Acts* 10.42; 17.31; 2 *Cor* 5.10]. By
immediately adding, 'and by his appearing and his kingdom', Paul shows that he expected the day of universal
judgment to coincide with Christ's glorious appearing and
the consummation of his kingdom. It is clear from verse
18 that the goal which Paul has in view is the heavenly
kingdom, and not an earthly millennium! The appearing
'is for all men alike, the kingdom is for the blessed alone'
(Lenski). The five imperatives which follow summon
Timothy to the urgent fulfilment of his duty.

preach the word; Timothy's primary task is to preach
the gospel, and this is the first duty of every minister [1
Cor 9.16, 17]. The word is the objective deposit of truth
which is entrusted to the man of God [1.14]. He is not to
give the people stones instead of bread, by publishing his
own opinions or delivering lectures in philosophy – not
even 'Christian' philosophy! His task as a herald of God's
grace means that he must preach the word, the whole
word, and nothing but the word [*Acts* 20.27]. The remaining imperatives show how this great work is to be done.

be urgent in season, out of season; 'that is, at all times;
for what may seem to the careless or lukewarm unseason-
able occasions for making mention of the truth, will often
by the zealous and faithful pastor be found opportunities
of usefulness' (Fairbairn).

reprove, rebuke, exhort, with all longsuffering and

teaching. As there can be no healing without hurting, the preacher must make it his aim to convict the conscience and rebuke the sin of his hearers before encouraging them with the comforts of the gospel [*Jer* 8.11]. In each aspect of this ministry, he must show himself to be a sound teacher of the word, by bringing the truth to bear upon the particular circumstances of his people. And he is also to do it 'with all longsuffering', neither losing patience with them nor despairing of their salvation.

V 3: **For the time will come when they will not endure the sound doctrine; but, having itching ears, will heap to themselves teachers after their own lusts; 4 and will turn away their ears from the truth, and turn aside unto fables.**

Paul urges Timothy to be diligent in proclaiming the truth, because he foresees that the time will come when men will not put up with 'the sound doctrine' [see comment on 1 *Tim* 1.10]. But they will be driven by their own desires to accumulate for themselves teachers who will tickle their 'itching ears', i.e. ears 'which were always pricking with an uneasy desire for what would gratify the taste of a carnal, self-willed heart' (Fairbairn). This explains why the truth so seldom gets a hearing. Such people refuse to listen to it, and prefer to turn aside to empty myths. They delight to hear 'fables, any idle stories, or impertinent discourses, provided they touch not their lusts' (Poole).

V 5: **But be thou sober in all things, suffer hardship, do the work of an evangelist, fulfil thy ministry.**

In contrast to those who are intoxicated by error, Timothy must retain that clarity of mind and sound judgment which will enable him to persevere in his God-given calling without faltering. This will mean accepting the hardship which is involved in doing the work of an evangelist, i.e. preaching the gospel. With Paul's example before him [*vv* 6–8], he must not allow the prospect of suffering to deter him from fulfilling his ministry. 'Timothy is exhorted to make actual the potentialities of his ministry with the utmost whole-heartedness' (Simpson).

V 6: **For I am already being offered, and the time of my departure is come.**

In drawing attention to the beauty of Paul's 'swan-song' [*vv* 6–8], Findlay says that no passage in his Epistles is more finely touched with the apostle's genius. 'These verses have an ideal fitness as the apostle's final record and pronouncement upon his own career . . . Nor has Christian faith since found any higher expression of its sense of victory in the presence of death'. 'As for me' (NEB) does more justice to Paul's emphatic 'for I', since the phrase tacitly reminds Timothy of the urgent need to redouble his efforts now that Paul has reached the end of his ministry. What was contemplated as a possibility in *Phil* 2.17 is now a certainty, and Paul's life is already being poured out like a drink offering upon God's altar [cf *Num* 15.1–10]. It would appear from *Rom* 15.16 that Paul regarded his mission to the Gentiles in terms of an offering to God, and now that sacrificial service will be completed by his approaching death. The metaphorical use of such cultic imagery must not be pressed; it clearly does not mean that Paul is offering some kind of secondary atone-

2 TIMOTHY, CHAPTER 4, VERSE 6

ment. The word 'departure' was used of loosing a ship from its moorings, or of a soldier striking his tent, but probably neither image is in view here as the word was a common euphemism for death. What this departure meant for Paul is vividly conveyed in *Phil* 1.23, where he speaks of his 'desire to depart and be with Christ; for it is very far better'.

V 7: **I have fought the good fight, I have finished the course, I have kept the faith:**

The imminence of Paul's departure enables him to look back on the long contest in which he has been engaged from the vantage point of victory. 'I have fought the good fight' recalls 1 *Tim* 6.12 (see comment there), and refers to his success in contending for 'the prize of the high calling of God in Christ Jesus' [*Phil* 3.14]. This is placed first because Paul is a Christian before he is an apostle [*v* 8]. 'I have finished the course' continues the athletic metaphor, though the figure is changed from the wrestling-match to the race [cf 1 *Cor* 9.26]. Paul's life-long ambition is at last fulfilled now that he has completed his course of Christian service [*Acts* 20.24]. With the final member of this triad Paul drops the metaphor and states the literal fact: 'I have kept the faith'. He has guarded and transmitted intact the sacred deposit of the gospel [1.14]. 'Through all trial, and mockery, and persecution, and suffering, he had held fast by the saving truths which he received by special revelation from above, and which as a chosen vessel he was sent forth to declare to a perishing world' [*Gal* 1.12; *Acts* 9.15] (Fairbairn).

V 8: **henceforth there is laid up for me the crown of**

[163]

righteousness, which the Lord, the righteous judge, shall give to me at that day; and not to me only, but also to all them that have loved his appearing.

Having now finished his course, Paul only has to await the due reward of his labours, which the Lord the righteous judge will give to him 'at that day', i.e. the day of Christ's appearing. The crown is the recompense for a righteous life; 'it is that kind and measure of bliss which the wrestler in righteousness alone is either entitled or prepared to enjoy' (Fairbairn). A comparison of this verse with 1 *Cor* 9.25 would suggest that 'the crown of righteousness' is to be identified with the 'incorruptible' crown of eternal life. But the promised 'reward' nevertheless remains a divine donation, and must be received as a gift, because all Paul's work is the fruit of God's grace [1 *Cor* 15.10]. Moreover, this gift of eternal life is not for Paul alone, but for all who 'have loved his appearing'. Such a love for Christ's return affords the only adequate motivation for living righteously in this present evil age [1 *John* 3.2, 3]. 'The perfect tense is used because their love will have continued up to the moment of their receiving the crown' (White).

*V*9: **Give diligence to come shortly unto me: 10 for Demas forsook me, having loved this present world, and went to Thessalonica; Crescens to Galatia, Titus to Dalmatia.**

In these closing sentences Paul outlines his present circumstances without a trace of self-pity, but there is deep pathos in the last picture they give us of the great apostle [*vv* 9–18]. As he awaits the final crisis in his cold, cheerless dungeon, he longs to see his 'beloved child' once more.

Timothy must do his best to come quickly, because Paul is almost alone, following the desertion of Demas to Thessalonica, and the departure of Crescens to Galatia and Titus to Dalmatia (now Yugoslavia). Evidently Crescens and Titus were despatched to do the Lord's work, but Demas deserted Paul because he gave up the love of Christ's appearing for the love of this present world [*v* 8].

*V*11: **Only Luke is with me. Take Mark, and bring him with thee; for he is useful to me for ministering. 12 But Tychicus I sent to Ephesus.**

Luke very likely acted as Paul's secretary in taking down this Epistle. 'The faithful Luke bides still with the age-worn apostle, to whom he could best minister in his painful weakness and suspense. His comradeship must have been the bright spot in the encircling gloom of his close captivity. There is a tremulous note in the *only*' (Simpson). Timothy is also to pick up Mark and bring him to Rome, for Paul had long since changed his opinion of Mark and now finds him useful in the ministry [*Acts* 13.13; 15.38; *Col* 4.10; *Philemon* 24]. 'I sent' is probably the epistolary aorist, 'I am sending'. If so, it identifies Tychicus as the bearer of the letter and suggests that Paul was sending him to Ephesus to supervise the work there during Timothy's absence.

*V*13: **The cloak that I left at Troas with Carpus, bring when thou comest, and the books, especially the parchments.**

With winter approaching [*v* 21], Paul feels the need for the heavy cloak which he left at Troas with Carpus, and he asks Timothy when he comes to bring this together with his books and precious parchments. Perhaps these writings included parts of the Greek Old Testament, and collections of the Lord's sayings which Paul may have wished to hand on to Luke [*Luke* 1.1–4]. Be that as it may, it is clear that Paul desired to make good use of whatever time was left to him by continuing his reading and study. Paul's request may be aptly compared with that made by William Tyndale from his damp cell to the governor of Vilvorde Castle. He begged for a warmer cap and cloak, a woollen shirt, but 'most of all my Hebrew Bible, Grammar and Vocabulary, that I may spend my time in that pursuit'.

V 14: **Alexander the coppersmith did me much evil: the Lord will render to him according to his works: 15 of whom do thou also beware; for he greatly withstood our words.**

Paul here recalls a specific occasion when he suffered a great deal of harm through this man's implacable opposition to the gospel in order to warn Timothy to be on his guard against him. Since we know nothing further about 'Alexander the coppersmith', the nature of his offence remains a matter of conjecture. Perhaps he had been instrumental in securing Paul's re-arrest (Simpson), or he may have been the leading witness for the prosecution at Paul's first hearing in Rome (Lenski). But Paul is content to leave the issue in higher hands, for 'the Lord will render to him according to his works' [*Deut* 32.35; *Rom* 12.19]. Although this is a prediction and not an imprecation, the certainty of the Lord's judgment upon such an adversary of the truth caused Paul no distress. 'If God is a moral governor; if sin is a reality; those who know themselves to be on God's side cannot help a feeling of joy in knowing that evil will not always triumph over good' (White).

V16: At my first defence no one took my part, but all forsook me: may it not be laid to their account.

Paul sadly records that at the preliminary investigation (*prima actio*), which preceded the trial proper in Roman law (*secunda actio*), no one had the courage to speak up for him in court. All the Christians in Rome deserted him in his hour of need, but he forgives their failure and prays that it may not be held against them [*Luke* 23.34; *Acts* 7.60]. 'He would have it to be reckoned as a proof of weakness, not of false-heartedness' (Fairbairn).

V17: But the Lord stood by me, and strengthened me; that through me the message might be fully proclaimed, and that all the Gentiles might hear: and I was delivered out of the mouth of the lion.

In contrast to the failure of his friends, Paul triumphantly affirms the faithfulness of the Lord, who stood by him and imparted the strength which enabled him to bring his ministry to its completion in the capital of the pagan world. Paul did this by preaching the gospel to the vast throng of Gentiles who had come to hear the trial, which was probably held in one of the large basilicas in Rome. 'We annex a territory by the mere act of planting our country's flag on a small portion of its soil; so in St. Paul's thought a single proclamation of the gospel might have a spiritual, almost a prophetical, significance, immeasurably greater than could be imagined by one who heard it'

(White). Paul's inspired 'apologia' made such a deep impression upon the court that he was rescued from the lion's mouth. Presumably the expression is an oblique reference to his temporary reprieve from Nero's malice. 'After his first examination Paul could still write to Asia bidding Timothy and Mark come to him, which shows that he looked forward to a considerable interval before the next stage of his trial' (W. M. Ramsay, *St. Paul the Traveller and the Roman Citizen*, p. 361).

*V*18: **The Lord will deliver me from every evil work, and will save me unto his heavenly kingdom: to whom *be* the glory for ever and ever. Amen.**

Paul knows that he has reached the end of his earthly course [*v* 7], and does not expect to be acquitted at his next appearance in court. But past deliverances assure him that the Lord will rescue him from every evil work and bring him safely to his heavenly kingdom. The machinations of the Evil one and his human agents can inflict no abiding harm upon one who enjoys Christ's protection. 'Christ's kingdom here on earth is where he rules with his grace and his gospel; Christ's heavenly kingdom is where he rules with heavenly glory' (Lenski). As Paul joyfully anticipates his transfer to that state of bliss [*Phil* 1.23], he ascribes all the glory to Christ in a fervent doxology which he seals with an emphatic 'Amen'. 'The very hope produces a doxology: how much more the realization!' (Bengel).

*V*19: **Salute Prisca and Aquila, and the house of Onesiphorus.**

Paul sends greetings to his staunch friends and fellow-workers, Prisca and Aquila, the much travelled Jewish couple [*Acts* 18.2], who are evidently back in Ephesus again [cf *Rom* 16.3]. Prisca is usually named first, and this may indicate her great ability. Paul also greets the household of Onesiphorus, because he knew that Onesiphorus was not with his family when this letter was written [see comment on 1.16–18].

*V*20: **Erastus remained at Corinth: but Trophimus I left at Miletus sick.**

This Erastus is probably the companion of Timothy mentioned in Acts 19.22. Trophimus was the innocent cause of the Temple riot in Jerusalem which led to Paul's first arrest [*Acts* 21.29]. It is not without contemporary significance that an apostle with the gift of healing left unhealed an associate who was sick! As Simpson notes, 'Miracles of healing were not at the command of their performers. There may be a reason in the divine counsels for a believer's sickness as well as for his health'.

*V*21: **Give diligence to come before winter. Eubulus saluteth thee, and Pudens, and Linus, and Claudia, and all the brethren.**

Paul makes a last appeal for Timothy to do his best to come before the winter, and sends the greetings of four Roman Christians who are otherwise unknown to us, unless Linus is the man who was to become bishop of Rome. Probably none of them had sufficient standing in the city to support Paul in court [*v* 16]. As for the rest, his heart is large enough to account them 'brethren' still.

[169]

V22: **The Lord be with thy spirit. Grace be with you.**

These are the last words of the great apostle. He first prays that the Lord may be with Timothy's spirit, and then embraces all believers in the final benediction, 'Grace be with you all!' (NEB). Paul thus ends his ministry on the same note with which it began [*Acts* 13.43], for what was his 'signature' in every Epistle is also his final prayer for the church [2 *Thess* 3.17, 18].

Soli Deo Gloria

BIBLIOGRAPHY

Arndt, W. F., and Gingrich, F. W., *A Greek-English Lexicon of the New Testament* (University of Chicago Press, 1957)

Barrett, C. K., *The Pastoral Epistles* (OUP, 1963)

Beasley-Murray, G. R., *Baptism in the New Testament* (Paternoster Press, 1972)

Bengel, J. A., *New Testament Word Studies* (Kregel, 1971)

Bernard, J. H., *The Pastoral Epistles* (CGT) (CUP, 1899)

Bruce, F. F., *Paul: Apostle of the Free Spirit* (Paternoster Press, 1977)

Bruce, F. F., *Expanded Paraphrase of the Epistles of Paul* (Paternoster Press, 1965)

Calvin, John, *The Epistles to Timothy and Titus* (St. Andrew Press, 1964)

Earle, Ralph, *1, 2 Timothy* (EBC) (Zondervan, 1978)

Ellis, E. Earle, *Paul and his Recent Interpreters* (Eerdmans, 1961)

Erdman, Charles R., *The Pastoral Epistles* (Westminster Press, 1966)

Fairbairn, Patrick, *The Pastoral Epistles* (James and Klock, 1976)

Gaffin, Richard B., *The Centrality of the Resurrection* (Baker Book House, 1978)

Gasque, W. Ward, and Martin, Ralph P. (Editors), *Apostolic History and the Gospel* (Paternoster Press, 1970)

Giesler, Norman L. (Editor), *Inerrancy* (Zondervan, 1979)

Guthrie, Donald, *The Pastoral Epistles and the Mind of Paul* (Tyndale, 1956)

Guthrie, Donald, *The Pastoral Epistles* (TNTC) (Tyndale, 1957)

BIBLIOGRAPHY

Guthrie, Donald, *New Testament Introduction* (Tyndale, 1970)

Hendriksen, William, *I & II Timothy and Titus* (Banner of Truth, 1957)

Henry, Matthew, *Commentary on the Holy Bible* (various editions)

Hiebert, D. Edmund, *First Timothy* (Moody Press, 1957)

Hiebert, D. Edmund, *Second Timothy* (Moody Press, 1958)

Hiebert, D. Edmund, *Titus & Philemon* (Moody Press, 1957)

Hiebert, D. Edmund, *Titus* (EBC) (Zondervan, 1978)

Hinson, E. Glenn, *1–2 Timothy and Titus* (BBC) (Broadman Press, 1971)

Humphreys, A. E., *The Epistles to Timothy and Titus* (CBS & C) (CUP, 1895)

Huther, J. E., *The Pastoral Epistles* (Meyer NTC) (T & T Clark, 1881)

Kelly, J. N. D., *The Pastoral Epistles* (A & C Black, 1963)

Kent, Homer A., *The Pastoral Epistles* (Moody Press, 1958)

Kittel, G. and Friedrich, G., *Theological Dictionary of the New Testament* Vols. I–X (Eerdmans, 1964–76) (Translated by Geoffrey W. Bromiley: Index by Ronald E. Pitkin)

Knight, George W., *The Faithful Sayings in the Pastoral Epistles* (Presbyterian & Reformed, n.d.)

Ladd, George E., *The Blessed Hope* (Eerdmans, 1956)

Lenski, R. C. H., *The Interpretation of Paul's Epistles to Timothy and Titus* (Augsburg, 1961)

Lock, Walter, *The Pastoral Epistles* (ICC) (T & T Clark, 1966)

Metzger, Bruce M., *A Textual Commentary on the Greek New Testament* (United Bible Societies, 1971)

Morris, Leon, *Ministers of God* (IVP, 1968)

Morris, Leon, *The Apostolic Preaching of the Cross* (Tyndale, 1965)

Murray, John, *The Collected Writings* Vol. I (Banner of Truth, 1976)

Murray, John, *Principles of Conduct* (Tyndale, 1957)

Parry, R. St. John, *The Pastoral Epistles* (CUP, 1920)

Pink, Arthur W., *Gleanings from Paul* (Moody Press, 1967)

Poole, Matthew, *Commentary on the Holy Bible* Vol. 3 (Banner of Truth, 1963)

Ramsay, W. M., *St. Paul the Traveller and the Roman Citizen* (Hodder & Stoughton, 1900)

Robertson, A. T., *Word Pictures in the New Testament* Vol. IV (Broadman Press, 1931)

Sabatier, A., *The Apostle Paul – Appendix on the Epistles to Timothy and Titus by G. G. Findlay* (Hodder & Stoughton, 1903)

Saucy, Robert L., *The Church in God's Program* (Moody Press, 1972)

Shedd, W. G. T., *Dogmatic Theology* (Klock & Klock, 1979)

Simpson, E. K., *The Pastoral Epistles* (Tyndale Press, 1954)

Stott, John R. W., *Guard the Gospel* (IVP, 1973)

Taylor, Thomas, *An Exposition of Titus* (Christian Classics, n.d.)

Trapp, John, *Commentary on the New Testament* (Sovereign Grace Book Club, 1958)

Trench, R. C., *Synonyms of the New Testament* (James Clarke, 1961)

Vincent, Marvin R., *Word Studies in the New Testament* (MacDonald, n.d.)

Vine, W. E., *Expository Dictionary of New Testament Words* (Oliphants, 1958)

Warfield, B. B., *The Person and Work of Christ* (Presbyterian & Reformed, 1950)

Warfield, B. B., *The Inspiration and Authority of the Bible* (Marshall Morgan & Scott, 1959)

Warfield, B. B., *Faith and Life* (Banner of Truth, 1974)

Warfield, B. B., *The Lord of Glory* (Evangelical Press, 1974)

White, Newport J. D., *The Epistles to Timothy & Titus* (EGT) (Eerdmans, 1974)

Yamauchi, Edwin, *Pre-Christian Gnosticism* (Tyndale, 1973)